War on the Prairie

War on the Prairie

Carrie Ehlert Newman

NORTH STAR PRESS OF ST. CLOUD, INC.
SAINT CLOUD, MINNESOTA

Acknowledgements

I'd like to thank my Dad for instilling in me a love of history. I'd like to thank Corinne, Seal, and Brandon at North Star Press for correcting my grammar, teaching me so patiently and for taking a chance with me. Thank you!

ISBN: 978-0-87839-603-0

First Edition: September 2012

Printed in the United States of America

Published by
North Star Press of St. Cloud, Inc.
P.O. Box 451
St. Cloud, Minnesota 56302

www.northstarpress.com

www.northstarpress.com   Facebook - North Star Press

This book is dedicated to Joseph and Jonathan,
for giving their Mom time to write.

my Dad, for instilling a love of history in me.

Thank you Mom, Bethany and Gretchen. Thank you for everything!

Table of Contents

Chapter 1

Eggs Start a War

"EGGS?" WINONA SCREAMED at her brother, Brown Wing. "You killed someone over *eggs*? You idiot! A *C'aponka* is what you are! How could you do this?" Winona grabbed him by the shoulders, forcing Brown Wing to look her in the eyes.

"You have no idea what happened. You weren't there." Brown Wing sneered at her. "They were attacking *us*, shaming the Dakota ways. We had to. Our honor was at stake. Girls know nothing of honor." With that, Brown Wing flung her hands off him, spun around, gave her one final glare and sped off to join the men gathering by the fire.

"There's more to honor than killing someone!" Winona screamed after him. She fought to gain control over her emotions. There was so much shouting. If everyone shouted, who would listen? The entire village it seemed had gathered in front of her family's teepee. Her mother busily added more wood to the fire, so the men could see and talk. The men were arguing. Everyone, it seemed, was upset. As she walked to the fire, she could hear that some of the chiefs wished to give up the braves for their rash actions. Others, however, wished to follow up with another attack. Both sides were loud, louder than Winona had ever heard a council argue before.

Winona's father, Chief Red Middle Voice rose. He waited for quiet, then announced as loudly as he could, "These four young braves are heroic in what they have done, but there will be consequences. Last year we turned over a brave from the Winnebago tribe to the soldiers. The brave had killed a man and wanted us to hide him. We knew this was not right, so we turned him over to the white soldiers. The whites did not praise us. They did not reward us. In fact we were punished for hiding him."

"Yes, that is true." Wapai interrupted, "What Chief Red Middle Voice is saying is right. But we did hide the Winnebago brave. We hid him for days before we reached our decision. The whites were mad that we hid him, not that we turned him over. They cut our annuity payments. When they hear of this incident, they will stop all payments. We cannot hide these four braves. We cannot deliberate even more than this one moment. We must turn them over tonight. The white men demand swift justice."

Winona held her breath. To interrupt a chief while he spoke was a terrible mistake. It was more than rude. The tribe waited to see what Chief Red Middle Voice would say next.

"I thank you, Wapai, for reminding us of what is at stake. And I agree we must make a quick decision. Do we turn these young braves over to the white justice as Wapai suggests? Or do we use this as the young warriors among you insist? Do we go to war? No one planned for this to happen. But it has happened. We are all upset. Our brethren must support whatever decision is made. But this is too big of a decision for one band, for one chief, to make. We must be united in what we decide, for we all will suffer if it goes badly. We need all Dakota to be united, not just our band. We must go tonight to Chief Shakopee, and if Chief Shakopee agrees, we will ride to Chief Taoyateduta. The whites will demand vengeance. The chiefs must decide what is best together."

For a moment, Chief Red Middle Voice paused to let his words sink in. The wild war talk did not immediately return. Clearly all were realizing the gavity of the situation. Into the silence he spoke, "Two white women have been killed. This is a grave problem. We need council and agreement. The white retribution for this act will be swift and hard." After speaking, Chief Red Middle Voice did not wait for more talk. He stood and strode to his horse.

Wapai and the others who had been arguing to turn over the troublemakers also broke from the fire, going for their own horses. The young warriors leaped up, whooping. All chiefs would be listened to at Chief Shakopee's council, but they had to be there to be heard.

Winona's anger spilled over her again, as the village buzzed with excitement. Some faces expressed the rage Winona felt while others looked more fearful and concerned. Some looked eager for a fight. Still, most ran to help the braves mount their horses to ride to Chief Shakopee's village. Her brother tossed her a second wicked look and mounted his stolen horse. The four braves had stolen horses in Acton to ride quickly back and tell what they had done.

Winona remembered their arrival in the village late that afternoon. She had seen fear in their faces then. She remembered, too, his hastily told tale and the embarrassment he had felt, about what he had done. But, as the story was told again, and then again, the embarrassment and fear had been replaced with false bravery all too quickly. The four young men started to think they might not be punished but treated as heroes. Winona could not help herself. She hurled more insults after him. Perhaps he had the village and their father tricked, but Winona knew he was not brave. He had no honor. He had killed because his friends had made fun of him.

Her brother had always hated to be seen as foolish, and what he told of the event confirmed this. He would tell this story again to Chief Shakopee. Perhaps he would tell it again to Chief Taoyateduta. Winona could only imagine how Brown Wing's story would grow each time he told it until, finally, he'd leave out altogether that the white lady had chased him with a broom for trying to steal her eggs. A broom. Her brother had killed a woman for shaming him with a broom!

Winona had to stop screaming. Hurling insults at her brother was using up all her breath and making running harder. All the braves were far out of sight. Even those on foot could run faster than Winona. Winona used to be a fast runner. But months of hunger had taken their toll. Her brother and his friends had no such problem. If there was meat, Mother gave it to Brown Wing. Throughout the village this was common. Fathers insisted the braves eat first before the rest of the family ate.

"They must be strong. They have to protect us all," her father said every night, ignoring the hunger in his daughter's face.

"Against what," Winona asked, "starving?"

Her father never answered. He stared into the fire to remind Winona she was impertinent. "How does a warrior fight starvation?" Winona muttered as she stumbled along in the moonlight. She kicked at every rock and root she could see, and tripped over the ones she could not.

Winona forced herself to stop gritting her teeth. She felt so much anger at what had happened. But she could do nothing about it. She would not be listened to, for she was just a young girl. Tears of frustration spilled from her eyes, and she hastened to swipe at them with her braids. It would do no good to look like a crying girl when she reached Shakopee's.

Too impatient to walk, Winona broke into a run stopping only when the pain in her side grew too great. She desperately wanted to get to the war council at Shakopee's village and hear what was said. The other women and girls in her village were content to sit and gossip about what had been said. They would wait until the braves came back with their news.

Winona could not bear to sit still. She had to move, even if she had to move slower than she would like. As she walked, she kept going over the story in her head. Eggs, all of this was because of eggs? Killing, shouting, death. All for a handful of eggs? No, she suddenly realized. It wasn't about eggs. It was about being a man, but not being treated like one. This had nothing to do with eggs.

She walked and thought. She thought of what her brother had told her father. He and his three friends had gone hunting. The young braves did this often now. Food was so short that every little bit made a difference. The drought from last year made everything harder. The Dakota were no longer self-sufficient. They had become dependent on the government's annuity payments.

The treaty selling Dakota lands to the Great Father in Washington had been signed when Winona was just a baby. She herself had no memory of a life before yearly payments, before government promises of gold, food, schools, and missionaries sent from Washington to teach the Dakota to be more civilized. The Dakota had sold most of their land to the Great Father in Washington with the promise of care and gold.

It usually worked out well enough. But this year the hunger was worse. This year the annuity payments were very late. Winona, as well as the rest of her band, went to sleep hungry night after night. With hunting so poor, they depended on the payments to hold them from hunger until the gardens were ready in the fall.

This summer the hunters had been having terrible luck. *That's not unusual,* Winona thought. However, she was not foolish enough to say it in front of her brother and his friends. But their hunting trip had turned into something no one had expected. It was something Winona feared would change everything.

Winona arrived at Shakopee's village long after the riders. The men from her father's village were already in place, circled around the fire. The fire had been built up into a great council fire. She could see the faces of the men in the flickering firelight. Winona circled the group. She kept to the shadows, trying not to be seen, but wishing to hear. Winona wished to watch the face of Chief Shakopee, as he was told of what was done. All the men kept their emotions hidden. But, Winona wondered if she might see horror or revulsion in Chief Shakopee's face. She saw that most of Shakopee's band had gathered to hear the news.

As she quietly circled, Winona checked that her knife was still strapped to her thigh. Her father had given it to her two moons ago. She had made a sheath for it out of leather and kept it tied to her leg always. Her mother had helped her cut a small hole in the seam of her split wool skirt to be able to get it out without anyone knowing. She thanked her mother as she rubbed the bone handle in an attempt to calm her mind.

Winona could see that some of the men were excited to hear the story. Their faces showed a longing for the days of counting coup on enemies and the retelling of bold deeds. Other faces showed concern. Perhaps they thought of the retribution that would be demanded.

Red Middle Voice started to speak. "I ask these braves to tell of their story. Please listen so we all can hear what they have done."

As the boys spoke, Winona let her mind drift. She was most upset that they had killed two women. This was not the Dakota way. This was not brave. Women and children were to be protected. She had heard stories from her mother. If fighting came to their village, a trench was dug to protect the young and their mothers.

Winona hoped Chief Shakopee would chastise the braves for the death of a woman. She hoped it would end with the braves forced to turn themselves in or flee to western tribes. What if the braves had been hunting by her friend Margaret's farm? What if they had killed her and her mother? Not all whites were like the agents who cheated them and lied!

The angry voices of the tribe pulled her out of her musings. They were arguing. The elders were angry at women being killed just as Winona was. They said this was wrong. The whites would punish all Dakota if the young braves were not turned over immediately. Many of the older Dakota men nodded their heads at this. The young men did not. The braves in her band wished for war. They spoke louder, insisting that the time for war was now, while the white men were away fighting their other war. Finally, Chief Red Middle Voice rose again. Winona knew that he wished he had painted his face and dressed his hair with feathers, but it was all happening too fast. Still, even without his chief regalia, he would be listened to.

"My brothers. We are all upset that a white family has been killed. It was not the braves who did this, but their anger. We have been angry all summer. No, we have been angry much longer. We have been angry since the white man came, and we treated with him. He has called us brother. But he has not treated us as brothers. We call him Father. But he has not treated us, as a father should. He has taken our hands in peace. But he has done so with a knife hiding in his other hand. We have sold our land to his agents, but he has not remembered his promise to take care of us.

"In this, the harvest moon, we should be feasting and working to get foods stored for the cold months. Instead the corn dries on the stalk, too green and too sickly to be eaten, though many have tried."

Red Middle Voice paused and directed his eyes to the younger ones in the audience. He spotted Winona and stared at her until she ducked her head in shame. The green corn had made her very ill, as it had made all those who ate it, but what else was there to eat?

"My brothers, we have met with the agents again and again. We ask them to open the locked storage rooms and allow us to eat the food our Great White Father has sent for us. But they have refused and told us to leave. Soldiers arrived with their loaded howitzers. These they pointed at us to remind us that we should listen to those who have the large guns. My brothers, the agents will not listen to us. They do not treat us as we would treat them. Our young men say this is no longer working. We cannot sit and talk each day and return to our cook fires with nothing to cook. We are not able to feed our children.

"This cannot be what the Great White Father wants. Or is it? His agents work for him. Perhaps he has planned for us to die here on the prairie and open more land for the bad speakers? I know not what is in his mind. He is in Washington. I was not invited to go and speak with him." Red Middle Voice paused and looked again at all who had gathered. They too had not been to Washington, when the last of their land was cut away.

He continued, "If the gold would come, we could all buy food from the stores at the agency. The gold and the warehouses of goods would be distributed as in the past. Our families would get what is owed them and then pay the agent what they owe. The gold was due over three moons ago. What could be taking so long? How far away can this Washington be, that they can send food, but not gold? They can send agents, but not gold. We starve. We wait. How long?"

Now he changed tactics. "What should we do with these men? How shall we make sure justice happens? What is justice now? My young braves did this. We know that killing of white women will bring anger. We will all be punished for what these four did." He paused here to look at each of the four braves. Each stared at the fire, heads bowed as if just now understanding the gravity of what they had done.

Chief Red Middle Voice continued, "I and my band are still true Dakota. We are Blanket Sioux. We get less gold, less food than your tribe does. We get less because we have not given up all the Dakota ways. I do not farm like a cut hair. I will not put on a vest and pantaloons. We are Dakota. We can fight. We fight well. But we will not win by ourselves. The time has come for all Dakota to make their decision about how they wish to live or die.

"I ask you, Chief Shakopee . . . I ask you, my brothers . . . what should we do? It is time for war. If we fight, we die as men.

If not, we starve like dogs in our teepees. How shall we live? How will we fight?" Red Middle Voice stopped speaking. He looked around him. Then he sat at his place of honor, by the fire.

"I do not agree with Red Middle Voice," Wapai said. "This is not the way to a better life. If we go to war, many Dakota will die. Some will be killed in battle. Others will will die later of starvation. The government will not honor their treaty. They will not pay us what is owed if we attack defenseless women and families. It is wrong to go to war. It is right to turn over these troublemakers tonight, before too much is lost."

All were quiet. Winona's mind drifted to times not long ago when game was plentiful, the fish many, and bushes were full of ripe berries. But the settlers liked berries and fish too. So many had come, so many homesteaders crowded into their old reservation. Too many children with tin pails all picking at the same time. Food became scarce. Without the payments, without the promises of the government, the old men had lost their followers. Red Middle Voice was listened to more than other chiefs. He had never trusted the whites. He had given up little of his ways. The braves believed him to be strong. The elders, like Wapai, believed him to be a troublemaker.

Chief Shakopee rose. "Chief Red Middle Voice is right. This is too much for my band to decide alone. This is too much for Chief Red Middle Voice to decide alone. It might be true, what Chief Red Middle Voice says. We might win. We are both strong bands. We have strong warriors." The chief paused, "If we do not win, the war will end in defeat and banishment for all our bands. For all Dakota. We must go to Chief Taoyateduta. He is wise. He will know what is best." With those words, Chief Shakopee strode out of the firelight to get his horse and ride to Taoyateduta's village.

Winona stood slowly. She brushed the dirt off her wool skirt and smoothed her short dress over her hips. She checked to make sure her knife was in its sheath, and that her small bag was tied to her waist. It would not help to lose anything. She followed the braves into the night. Her anger was gone, replaced with something else, a feeling of unease, of uncertainty. It felt as if the very air weighed her down. Joining a handful of women and girls from Shakopee's village, Winona walked along quietly in the direction of Chief Taoyateduta's village. There was little talk amongst the girls and women. This was not normal, but then nothing about tonight was as it should be. Most of the women would stay and await the decision at their village. But a few like Winona needed to go along. They would come back and start running bullets or breaking camp if the chiefs declared war. But for now, they, like Winona, followed the braves into the night.

Chapter 2

Margaret

EGGS? ARE YOU EVEN LISTENING to yourself? Are you honestly saying someone was killed over an argument about eggs?" Jakob sneered at Margaret.

Margaret pleaded with her brother. "I know, I know, it sounds crazy, but you should listen to Winona. She came to warn us. Winona says the Dakota chiefs have declared war. They plan on attacking, and we might be caught in the middle."

"Winona hopes the bands will follow Chief Taoyateduta, Little Crow, and not attack the agency. However, she's worried that some of the younger braves are too angry to follow their chief, like her brother, Brown Wing. You know what his anger's like." Jakob snorted loudly, forcing Margaret to pause and try again. "Winona's worried, Jakob. Please. I've never seen her this upset. She ran all night to warn us. She thinks the younger braves might attack the farmers. They've already killed two white women. She doesn't think we're safe. Would you please come with me and listen to her?"

"Why would they attack us?" Fear showed in Jakob's eyes for just a moment.

"Think, Jakob, just think a minute. You know what Brown Wing is like when he's mad. You know how his anger overtook him even when we were kids playing. If Brown Wing is at the cause of this, there'll be trouble. He hates you. He hates Father. If he's being listened to, the Dakota will attack the farms. I don't want to believe it, but they plan on attacking at daybreak. They could be attacking other farms right now. Winona thinks we should . . ."

Margaret suddenly realized she wasn't sure what Winona wanted them to do.

"I ain't going to listen to no Dakota. And certainly not a girl." Jakob's fear had turned to anger. He cleared his throat and spit on the ground next to Margaret's shoe. The long line of spittle left on his face spoiled the tough effect he was going for. "Get the milking done. I'm going to turn the oxen loose to graze. Pa's expecting us to get the chores done. Murdering savages or not, the cow needs milking! Then I'll go explain things to Ma." As he turned from Margaret, she could hear him muttering about eggs and troublemakers.

"You aren't the boss of me!" Margaret hollered to his back, but then ran for the barn before he could retaliate. "He thinks he's so tough just cause Pa left this morning. He's not so tough. He doesn't know what to do. He's just as scared as I am. Oh, but he has to act all high and mighty as if he knows something and I don't." Margaret continued to mumble until Mabel, the milk cow swished her tail at Margaret's head. Then Margaret stopped talking to herself and concentrated on milking. Should she even be taking the time to milk and do chores? How much time did they have?

Winona had arrived as dawn was breaking. The family had already been up for a while. Pa had left and Margaret was getting dressed for chores when she heard the bird call, a killdeer's call, by her window. Margaret looked out but could never see Winona, although she knew she was close, and Margaret rushed to meet her at their tree. Usually it meant something fun, but not this morning.

Margaret was speechless when she saw Winona. Winona was filthy and scared. Her short gown, a blouse really, was torn in places. Her braids were all mussed and had leaves and twisted twigs sticking out from where they had caught in her hair. It looked as if she had been crying; something Margaret had never seen Winona do before.

The fact that Winona had been crying scared Margaret almost more than what Winona told her next. Winona's words tumbled out. Margaret felt as if she were in a river's rapids. She tried to grab onto the words, but they didn't make sense. Winona finally took a breath and continued haltingly, "You and your family are not safe. Get them quick and bring them back here. We'll figure out something. The house and barn aren't safe."

"But Father's already gone." Margaret burst out, "He left this morning with Mr. Schwandt to bring the boys to jail or fight."

"Boys!" Winona choked. "Boys exactly! They think they are men, but they are just boys. Well, they have done it now. They have caused enough trouble for all of us."

After Winona finished, Margaret raced to the barn to tell Jakob. That had not gone well. Somehow when he yelled at her to do her chores, it made sense. To get their work done before . . . Well, before what! That was the problem. What could they do?

Even if Father were here, would he listen to Winona? He was so excited when their closest neighbor had ridden up to tell the news of the killings near Acton.

"I don't know all the details." Mr. Schwandt had said, "But I heard tell, the family wasn't expecting it. Unarmed, no guns, is what I heard."

Margaret's father replied, "I reckon they were drinking and forgot themselves and who's in charge around here. I'll ride with you north awhile and we'll see what's what." As her father saddled and mounted his horse, he told Jakob, "Son, you're in charge. See to things here. I'll be back as soon as this business is finished."

Jakob positively grew with those words. Their father was not known to give much to him by way of responsibility. He usually yelled at everything Jakob or Margaret did wrong. Nothing they ever did was good enough, according to him. Never before had he put Jakob in charge.

Margaret had wondered about what he said about the Dakota drinking while she started getting dressed to do her chores. Those who lived so close to the reservation knew that, since the payment was on its way, more whiskey was made available to the Dakota. The traders would drive better bargains for themselves if they liquored up the Dakota men first.

She knew it wasn't liquor. Eggs had started it. She could almost hear her father saying that no one shoots someone over eggs. Just like Jakob, he wouldn't believe Winona's story. Although, it was a lot to take in, it was the truth. Mr. Schwandt didn't know. Brown Wing had been there. He said it was about eggs. Winona was there when the Dakota started to talk of going to war. Yet her father would believe a white man who knew absolutely nothing, instead of listening to a Dakota girl who had heard the actual talk of war.

Margaret's father did not like the Dakota. He said this often and expected his family to share his belief. Jakob certainly did, but Margaret didn't believe all Dakota were savages. Mother didn't either, but she chose not to disagree with Father. Margaret tried not to, but her tongue sometimes had a mind of its own.

Father said the Dakota were too lazy to farm. They did not deserve this rich farmland by the Minnesota River. He said they should be driven out of the land entirely. Margaret tried to remind him that some Dakota did farm. They all wished to stay in their homeland. Some were learning how to farm the white man's way, and they were called farm Dakota. While others, traditional Dakota or blanket Sioux, wanted to keep their traditions of hunting. Margaret disagreed with her father but he never listened to her. Now she felt like screaming *See, Father, I was right. You should have listened to me! If I feel like screaming when I'm not listened to, what does a grown man feel? A chief feel?*

She wanted to scream at her brother. She wanted to scream at her absent father. At Mabel, the milk cow. Why would no one listen to her, or to a girl who had run all night? *Well, I could, Couldn't I? I could tell mother and help her get to where Winona was. Screaming won't make me be heard, but I could do something right now. I could go tell mother and get her to come out to Winona.*

She finished milking and put the stool away. She stopped for a minute outside the barn and stared in all directions. Things seemed normal. Her brother hollered to her. "Stop lollygagging, and get the chickens done!"

Oh, he was a fine one to tell someone else to get busy. Hiding from their father most days so he wouldn't have to work! Margaret put the pail of milk in the shade of the porch. Then she ran to feed the chickens and gather the eggs. She'd tell mother as soon as she had the eggs gathered. Eggs again!

Margaret hurried. Winona seemed to think war parties would be here any minute. It was time for her to do something and not wait for Jakob. Father was not here, but he would not have listened to her anyway. He would have patted her on the head and told her she could not possibly understand a man's business.

After gathering the eggs, she got a bucket of water from the well. Margaret knew mother would listen to her. But where should they go? Winona had not said.

Margaret thought they should go to Reverend Hinman at the Episcopal Mission. He believed in helping the Dakota. Winona and her mother went to his services. So did Chief Little Crow. The reverend spoke of the Dakota who needed the congregation's help to become Christian. Many of the Farm Dakota, attended his church. They believed in wearing white clothes and cutting their hair. They were giving up their old ways. The mission was where they should go, Margaret decided. Reverend Hinman would keep them safe.

Margaret was done with the chickens. It is time to do something. *Or will it be too late!* She put the basket of eggs over her arm and walked briskly to the house, thinking of the reverend and how her father always nodded during the service. He agreed with the reverend about all the Dakota needing to change. "A civilized man farms!" her father would say. "They do not let their women do all the work and complain it's the white's fault when they go hungry."

What does it matter? Margaret thought, as she hurried to the house. If a drought comes, it dries out everything. It hurts all. It hurts the farm Dakota, the blanket Sioux, and the white settlers. Last year the crops in neat rows wilted just as fast as ones grown in a tangled garden. People went hungry without those crops.

Still Margaret was not as hungry as Winona. Margaret's family could get credit at any store in Hutchinson, Forest City, or New Ulm. They didn't need to wait for government payments. Their word was enough to gain some flour and salted pork until harvest. Margaret's family paid the debt when their crop came in, or with next year's crop. Winona talked about traders who would not give the Dakota their flour and pork until the money was handed out. Food remained locked in a warehouse while people starved.

Margaret could not imagine her father shrugging his shoulders and saying this was how it had always been done if she and her brothers were starving. The Dakota were so hungry. They were thin and gaunt. Many seemed too listless to care for themselves or their children. Her father used this as more proof that the Dakota were lazy. Starving was different than laziness, Margaret wanted to explain to her father, but he would have scolded her for talking back, so she kept her arguments safely in her head. It was better to avoid a whipping by staying quiet.

Eggs. It did make sense if you were hungry enough. If the store would not give you credit, if the money from the United States government was late again, and the food sat in a warehouse and you were not allowed to eat it. Would she hurt someone for food? She wasn't hungry like the Dakota were. If she were starving, what would she do?

Wearily, Margaret put her basket of eggs by the milk on the porch. She could hear her brother telling their mother everything he knew. Margaret needed to make sure he told the story correctly. She knew he wouldn't. He wouldn't tell of the braves. He wouldn't tell of the eggs or what Chief Little Crow had said. Her brother didn't know everything. He hadn't listened to her. But Margaret shook her head. Even if he knew the whole story, he wouldn't tell it. He'd tell only what he wanted Mother to hear.

Margaret worried her mother wouldn't listen to her story. She, too, wouldn't listen to what Winona said happened. With a shiver of fear, Margaret realized she had to get her mother to listen. They must leave at once. Margaret knew they weren't safe. Just like the animals that knew when a thunderstorm approached, Margaret could sense the danger even though she couldn't see it.

"Ma, I'm just telling you what I know. I think you'll be safe but I got to go to the agency. If the Dakota are attacking, they'll need every able bodied man to defend it!" Jakob held Father's old gun.

"I've got to go," Jakob continued. "You'll be fine here. Don't worry. The Dakota won't attack here. They're interested in the warehouses. Starving men will feed themselves and then worry about other things." Jakob spoke as if he understood men at war. Margaret might have laughed if his mistake didn't have such deadly implications.

Margaret couldn't stand it any longer. She stormed into the house, interrupting Jakob's misinformed goodbye speech. "Winona said we had to stay together. She thinks we need to leave the house. I think we should go see the reverend. He'll know what to do."

Her mother turned to her with a shocked look that affirmed Margaret's fears. Jakob had not told her much of anything. Margaret realized that Mother was not even remotely aware of the danger they were in.

Jakob's harsh reply was like a slap. "You can listen to some crazy, leather-legged girl if you want to. I'm gonna go do my duty. Pa would want this." Jakob stomped to the door.

"Pa told you to look after us. Not run out at the first sign of trouble!" Margaret shouted after him.

"I ain't running out." Jakob sneered, turning to glare at Margaret. "Trouble isn't coming here. Winona wants you to run into it. She might be trying to bring you back as her personal hostages or something. I reckon you'd better think why she'd come all this way if there was a war? Where are her loyalties? Why ain't she with her family and kin? You think she's here to protect you?" Jakob spat.

"You can't trust none of them Dakota. Ma, I'm telling you, for your own good. Stay here with Baby Isaac. Keep Margaret in her place. She's been listening to that no good Winona too much." With that he stormed out the door.

"What on God's green earth is going on?" Mother asked. "First your father leaves. Now Jakob is off to fight the Dakota. Are they even attacking? Has everyone been in the sun too long? I hope you know what's going on, because I think the men in this family have no idea. They are running about like chickens with their heads cut off. Please, Margaret, what's going on? What has Winona told you? We can't sit by if there is trouble elsewhere."

Margaret started to tell her mother everything she knew. She paced through the kitchen and front room, looking out the windows as she spoke. Mother had taken the breakfast biscuits out of the Dutch oven, but she made no effort to eat. She slumped into her rocking chair, nursing Isaac as she followed Margaret's rapid pacing with her eyes.

Margaret took a deep breath, and Winona's story tumbled out of her. She told Mother about the eggs, about Brown Wing, about Red Middle Voice. Finally, she gulped some air and relayed Winona's message about the danger they were in.

Her mother had not said a word this entire time. She did not interrupt, like Jakob, telling her it could not be about eggs. Margaret rushed through the story, fearing there would not be enough time to get all the words out. Time was running out. They had to leave. She felt sure that they would be safer at the missionary. Despite Jakob's opposing advice, Margaret had to convince Mother to take action.

Chapter 3

Taoyateduta's Village

BY THE TIME WINONA REACHED IT, Chief Taoyateduta's house was surrounded. He had a house made of brick built by the missionaries with government monies. It was better than many white farmers had. This was Taoyateduta's reward for choosing to live as a cut-hair, a farm Dakota. He had kept some of his ways—he still wore traditional clothes—but he had started to farm as a white man, attend church at the agency, and he slept in a bed instead of on a mat as most Dakota still did.

Taoyateduta had traveled east with the chiefs many years before. He had come back an older, more weary man. Winona's father called him a broken old man. Winona did not see it. His body might be old, but his eyes were sharp. He was leader of his tribe, and of many of the Dakota bands. His opinion of what the boys had done would determine the outcome.

Winona circled the house. A fire had been built up in front of the house, but the backyard was dark. The absence of light and people in the back made it easier for Winona to try and find out what was going on. Taking a chance, she pressed her face up against a windowpane. Taoyateduta was still in bed, he must have woken and allowed the chiefs to come in and speak while he sat in bed. She could see, but could not hear what the chiefs were saying. Frustrated, Winona turned and paced around the house again. A large crowd was gathered by the fire in the front.

Winona's head ached. Her teeth throbbed from grinding them in frustration. She knew better than to ask anyone what was happening. Better to stay in the shadows and listen. She had to keep herself silent. Women, especially a girl as young as herself, would not be listened to. Her father had allowed her to follow along. If she stepped out of her place, she knew he would send her home.

As Winona circled the crowd gathered by the fire, she noticed her brother and the young braves. A large group of young braves from Taoyateduta's band had gathered to listen to her brother's story. Winona sagged to the ground. With such a large and eager audience, the young men would relish sharing. They were starting to believe in their heroism, but deep down Winona felt they knew killing the women was an act of cowardice. At least her brother still behaved as if ashamed, excited but ashamed nonetheless. The crowd quieted as if on cue and Brown Wing spoke.

"We walked for a long time. Spread out but never in front of each other. We hoped to find some game, perhaps, a bird flushed from the prairie. We had no luck. The hunting was poor. Nothing could be found. As is always the case now when we hunt, the game was gone. The white farmer had already over hunted the land. He had taken the very best. Now he had taken everything."

Brown Wing looked over the crowd. Winona had to give him his due. He knew how to hold an audience with his words.

"We turned to start back to our village. But we walked slow and with heavy hearts. Our sisters and brothers were hungry. They depended on us and we had failed. We wished to stop, but we did not want to return empty-handed so we walked. We followed a fence along the road of wagon tracks. As we followed it, we found a nest. There were five small eggs in it.

"Breaking Up picked up the eggs carefully in his hands. He thought to bring them home to his family.

"'Do not take them,' I said, 'they belong to the white man and we will get into trouble.'" Brown Wing lowered his eyes. His fear of being called a coward, even here at Taoyateduta's village was real. Winona was close enough to see that his eyelids were trembling. His hand shook where he held his gun by his side. Winona's own eyes widened. *He is truly scared. He is scared that he will be turned in. Or that he will be banished for being a coward. Good, I am glad, he has put enough fear in us!*

Breaking Up then stood to tell his part in what was becoming a well-rehearsed act. "I threw the eggs down. I no longer cared if they broke. 'You dare to tell me not to take these?' I told Brown Wing. 'We who have eaten nothing all day? We should not eat these eggs that are by the road? Who says they belong to the whites?'" Breaking Up's voice rose as he shouted the next words to the crowd, just as he had shouted at his friend. "'It is you who are afraid of the white man. You are afraid to take an egg, but you are half-starved. You are afraid to take an egg, when they have taken all our land, all our hunting game, and all our fish! They do not pay us what we are owed. You are the coward, and I will tell everybody so.'"

Breaking Up ceased shouting and stood quietly. Brown Wing stood and continued the story. "I shouted at Breaking Up that I was not a coward. I was not afraid of the white man, and that I would show him I was not afraid. I said I would go to his house and kill him. I asked if any of my friends were brave enough to go with me? All three replied they were brave and they would come with me to see who was the bravest."

"We said we would go with you," Breaking Up and the two other braves said as they joined Brown Wing to stand and tell the rest of the story. "We walked up to the house," Breaking Up continued. "The daughter of Mr. Jones came to the door. She was sweeping her house. When she saw Brown Wing on the stairs of her home, she scolded him like a mother hen scolds its chicks. Then she made to brush him off the step and hit him with her broom. We laughed as Brown Wing ducked her blows. Brown Wing shouted, 'I am not afraid of you' as he ran off.

"We could hardly run after him we were laughing so hard. I was doubled over because my gut hurt from all the laughter. We called to each other. We said hurtful things of our friend Brown Wing's courage. I said he let that white lady hit him with a broom. I am not proud of what I said but laughter had overtaken me. As we ran stumbling into each other and laughing, Brown Wing ran back towards us. He rushed past us, wearing a face of hatred. 'I will show you I am not afraid!' he shouted to us as he ran towards the farmhouse. He jumped all the stairs as if they were not there and ran through the darkened doorway. We heard a yell. A broom fell to the floor. More yelling. We followed to the porch and peered in. There was Brown Wing, standing in the kitchen and demanding something to eat, something to drink. Mr. Jones was saying he had nothing but biscuits but he would go get something for us to drink. He walked out of his house and started walking east on the road. I stuffed two biscuits in my mouth and followed. Brown Wing came along, as did Killing Ghost and Runs Against Something When Crawling.

"Mr. Jones went to another farm. Two women and two men came out to meet him. They poured us a drink. I did not even taste mine. We asked if the men would like to have a shooting contest to see who was a better shot. The men agreed. We walked to a clearing and took turns. We, of course, were better."

Breaking Up grinned at these words, and those gathered to listen breathed a collective sigh of relief. Perhaps this was all of the story? Some whispered to others. The whites were mad they were bested in a shooting contest. Winona snorted, then felt her face flush. As if that would mean running to Taoyateduta's village in the darkest part of night? Could her people really be so foolish?

Breaking Up continued, "We reloaded quickly, while the white men made jokes about how poor their shots were. They did not reload. The white men invited us back to the shade of the porch to have a drink. Brown Wing said, 'Lead the way.'" Winona felt her neighbor gasp as she realized what was coming next.

Brown Wing took over, "I fired at the farmer's back. He fell without a sound. The other men looked back, but their last sight was four warriors pointing their guns at them. The other two men fell. Killing Ghost and Runs Against Something When Crawling are good shots. We reloaded while Breaking Up shot the farmer's wife. She kicked some but did not rise. We walked away without taking any more of their drink or food"

"Yes, but Brown Wing forgets" interrupted Killing Ghost. "On our return to the Jones's place, he went in and shot She Who Hits with Broom. Brown Wing proved today he is a man and will not be made a fool."

If the boys expected laughter or praise at this statement, they were mistaken. Taoyateduta had come out while they were talking, and he frowned at this prideful boasting. Those gathered at the fire made way for him to come forward to speak to all who had gathered. He was quiet for a long time.

Winona could hear the crackling from the fire. She could hear the gurgle of the stream. She could hear nothing from the prairie. It seemed to be holding its breath, like she was. As she waited, she felt as if all were holding their breath. All waited for Taoyateduta's words. So much, so many lives depended on this man's words. What would they be? Winona squeezed her hands shut, allowing the nails to dig into her palms. The pain helped her focus. She could not jump up and start yelling. She could do nothing but listen and watch and hope.

Taoyateduta watched the braves and their chiefs. His eyes scanned his people who gathered close. When he looked at

Winona, she felt pierced by his glance. He seemed to be able to see her thoughts and the turmoil she was in. Winona felt he understood. She breathed a sigh. Was it relief? Could he choose an action that would not hurt more Dakota, or more whites?

Taoyateduta could see that the braves were ready for war. He seemed reluctant to give them what they wanted. He continued his silence, forcing those gathered to shift in their stance. Forcing his people to breathe, to exhale and inhale. The silence lingered and pushed down on Winona. Just as she thought he would speak and condemn the young men for their actions, Red Middle Voice interrupted his quiet. "These four braves had the courage I lacked when I spoke with the Indian Agent Myrick."

The crowd shifted back as if they had been hit. Chief Taoyateduta should be speaking! Their outrage left them open mouthed as Chief Red Middle Voice continued. "These four braves had the courage I lacked when I tried to get more credit from the store. These four braves had the courage I lacked when I reminded the traders that the food in the bulging warehouses was due to me and should be distributed. At last I have found my courage. I have tried to do things the way the whites have asked. But no more.

"Why am I made to pay more for flour and pork than the white man? Why am I not given credit when the payment is late? I say I have had enough. I say the Dakota have had enough. It is time to choose to be men. I ask you, Chief Taoyateduta, to help the Dakota be strong enough, united enough to rid our lands of whites once and for all."

Wapai cut him off. "I am glad you found your courage Chief Red Middle Voice. It is important to have courage when you ask to lead us into death." Wapai's rage swelled. "Courage should be also about doing what is right. We have four men here. Four braves who killed those whose guns were unloaded. They are not courageous. They have done wrong. They will make us all suffer."

The gathered Dakota murmured, whispering to themselves. Both Wapai and Chief Red Middle Voice were talking of courage, yet both should be quiet. This was Chief Taoyateduta's fire. He should speak first. All rules seemed to have vanished tonight.

"Thank you Wapai for reminding us of what is at stake" Red Middle Voice continued. His voice eerily calm. "Let me also remind everyone of what the traders have told us. The traders say if a Dakota is hungry then he should eat grass."

"It is true," a voice near Winona hissed, "I heard the trader Myrick tell Chief Taoyateduta to eat grass if he was hungry."

"The Dakota are hungry." Chief Red Middle Voice stated, his voice rising to be heard over the crowds' mutterings. "We Dakota sold our land to the Americans. They pay late. The payment this year is later than anyone can remember. What if they have forgotten to pay? What if our annuity does not come? What if it comes but the traders take all of it to pay what we owe? How can pork, flour, and blankets be worth tens of gold dollars? They do not cost this much in New Ulm? They do not pay the high Dakota price if they are white. We cannot eat grass. We are men. We are not cattle."

The crowd murmured agreement. Winona's mind whirled. Everyone was angry. Everyone seemed to be listening to her father. He was building on their anger. Stoking it like a fire. It would flare up. Already, no one was following the rules. Chief Taoyateduta had not acknowledged Red Middle Voice. This was his fire. *We should be listening to Taoyateduta.*

Instead, Wapai spoke. "I agree, we cannot, will not, eat grass. Trader Myrick is wrong. He is a cheat. But we will not get our food or our payments if we go to war. Killing Myrick would make sense. Killing the family does not. They have not wronged us." Wapai looked at Brown Wing as he said this. "A broom does not shame a true warrior. A broom is not a cause for death. These four men must be turned over. We must tell the other agents, the Christian missionaries of what Myrick said. We must trust in the white justice. We will not win a war against them. We will lose."

"You are a coward. You have no Ohetika!" Chief Red Middle Voice said. He was not shouting but the anger in his voice chilled all those seated by the fire. "All who do not follow Dakota ways are without Ohetika."

These words sent a chill through Winona. Her father had gone too far. He was now accusing Wapai and Taoyateduta of being cowards. This was not something Taoyateduta could forgive. Sensing the enormity of the situation, the crowd was hissing condemnation all around her.

Chief Taoyateduta could not allow this accusation to stay. He got to his feet slowly. Wrapping his blanket around his shoulders, he held himself stiffly. His rage showed in his face. He had seen more, done more that Chief Red Middle Voice ever would.

"Taoyateduta is not a coward and he is not a fool . . ." The chief paused and looked at those who had gathered. He sighed as he continued,

"Braves, you are like little children; you know not what you are doing. You are full of the white man's devil-water. You are like dogs in the Hot Moon when they run mad and snap at their own shadows. We are only little herds of buffalo left scattered. The great herds that once covered the prairies are no more. See!—the white men are like locusts when they fly so thick that the whole sky is a snowstorm. You may kill one—two—ten; yes, as many as the leaves in the forest yonder, and their brothers will not miss them. Kill one—two—ten and ten times ten will come to kill you.

"Yes; they fight among themselves away off. But do you hear the thunder of their big guns? No. It would take you two moons to run down to where they are fighting, and all the way your path would be among white soldiers as thick as tamaracks in the swamps of the Ojibways.

"Yes; they fight among themselves, but if you strike at them they will all turn on you and devour you and your women and your little children just as the locusts in their time fall in the trees and devour all the leaves in one day. Braves, you are fools. You cannot see the face of your chief. Your eyes are full of smoke. You cannot hear his voice. Your ears are full of roaring waters. Braves, you are like children—you are fools. You will die like the rabbits when the hungry wolves hunt them in the hard moon. Taoyateduta is not a coward, he will die with you."

Winona had clenched her fists as she listened to Chief Taoyateduta. She worked her jaw, clenching and unclenching it so her teeth gnashed together. Someone, her brother no doubt started whooping and hollering. Others joined in. A chant started. "Kill the whites, Kill all the whites! Drive them off the prairie."

Winona backed from the crowd as quietly as she could. Raw terror overtook her and she had to fight the impulse to run. She had to warn Margaret. But she could not alert any of her band to what she was doing. Who knew where this would lead? The anger of the Dakota braves would spill from them and consume the entire prairie. Just like a fire, it would consume everything before burning itself out.

As Winona struggled to walk and act as if she were in control, she passed Wapai. His face mirrored her fear. He too walked in a determined manner. Perhaps he was on his way to save someone? Winona could not dwell on thoughts like these. *I have to get across the river and to Margaret before it's too late.*

Chapter 4

It's Time to Leave

MARGARET PAUSED FINALLY FINISHED with the story. Mother looked shocked and weak. Finally, her mother put Isaac down in his cradle and stood up. She opened her mouth to speak but words did not come out. Margaret knew that she had to make the next decision. It was time to go. She walked over to her Mother. "We must go. Gather the things you need for Isaac. We can't wait in this house. You know what the Dakota think of Pa. The Dakota may come here for revenge."

"But I don't understand why Myrick is doing this?" Mother asked. "He's married to a Dakota woman. Why would he want her to go hungry? Why would he want his own infant to go hungry? Margaret! Are you sure you heard Winona's words correctly? It doesn't make sense. Are you sure you're not allowing your imagination to take over? Jakob said we're not in danger. Your Pa wouldn't have left us if he felt we were in danger. The Dakota wouldn't hurt us, I've given them food on many occasions."

"Ma, I heard her. Come with me and see her. She's hiding at our tree. She'll tell you. Once you see her, you'll know. There's no trickery in her words. Don't let Jakob sway you against Winona." Margaret replied. She had not stopped pacing. She felt they had to get out of this house and soon. It seemed like they were in the open. Noticeable. The tree was safer. Margaret knew it. But how to get her mother to move?

Just then Winona burst into the kitchen looking terrified. Her face was bruised and filthy. Her braids, usually so neat, were twisted and messy. At this moment the reality of their situation hit Margaret's mother with a force strong enough to knock the solid woman back into her chair. "This can't be true. What you said. It's not really happening. Surely they wouldn't kill women?"

"They already have," Winona replied forcefully. "We have to leave now. Your house is too close to the agency. Chief Taoyateduta plans to attack the agency and Fort Ridgley today. This morning. But, I fear not all braves will go with his plans, my brother for instance. He and others might break into smaller war parties and attack the farms. Your farm is too close to the agency. We must leave."

"Winona's right, Ma. We have to go. Our farm's too close. The Dakota are starving. You know this. Even though you've given out food, it won't be enough to save us if a war party comes. Ma, you know Pa isn't well liked. He steals their game. Pa's wronged the Dakota. We haven't. But it won't matter. The braves are acting like Jakob when he gets mad. We'll be blamed for what Myrick said. We'll be hurt because of the actions of a few. Ma, we could be killed!"

As the horror of these words began to sink in, Margaret had to fight the desire to run and hide with every ounce of resolve she could muster. Somehow, despite the weakness in her knees that threatened to give way at any moment, she managed to regain a bit of courage. Speaking with a command she didn't know she possessed, Margaret declared, "We need to find someplace safe. The house isn't safe. We must go." Noticing her mother's hesitation, she continued, "Think of Isaac. We have to protect him."

Winona was through listening. She grabbed the pan of hot biscuits, turned it over onto a dishcloth and dumped the pork from the other pan right on top of them. She tied this into a bundle.

Winona handed this to Margaret. Then Winona reached into the cradle, gathered Isaac in his blankets and carried him out the door. This worked where words had not. Margaret's mother quickly followed her.

Margaret followed them out, grabbing the shawls from their hooks on the porch. Looking around one last time, she saw the pail of milk from this morning. It felt like a hundred years had passed since she milked the cows. Could it really have been just two hours ago? How could an entire life shift in such a short time? Well, there was no time to think on that now. Standing up straight and drawing her courage in close, Margaret tossed the shawls over her shoulder, grabbed the milk with her free hand, and stepped off into a very scary future.

With Isaac in her arms, Winona strode powerfully, never looking back, to their tree. When they had all sat down in the hiding place, Winona handed the baby to its mother and looked out across the prairie. Everyone sat quietly until Margaret leaned over and asked, "What are we waiting for? What do we do next?"

"I'm not sure. I feel something dangerous. Can't you hear it? Sense it? We are hidden here. No one can see us through the long grass. Let's wait a minute and watch without being watched."

As they waited, Margaret undid Winona's braids. Combing them out with her fingers, she re-braided Winona's hair and tied the ends with the old strips of leather. Then she used some spit on her apron to wipe Winona's face clean. Margaret sighed. She felt better looking at her friend now. Hopefully Winona felt better too.

Winona's eyes were closed. She was leaning her back against the tree. Margaret did not think she was asleep, but could not be sure. Winona was a bit like a whirly wind, she never seemed to need much rest.

Margaret felt the unease Winona was talking about. She'd felt it earlier too. She knew waiting made sense. They did not want to walk into a war party. But waiting was hard. She had not had a chance to tell Winona that she thought getting to the Missionary chapel made the most sense. It was important they were not seen by a war party if they tried to do this. What if Winona was wrong? What if all the bands were following Taoyateduta? If they were all attacking the agency, there would be no war parties out on the prairie? Too many questions, Margaret did not like this many questions, she liked to know the facts.

Her thoughts were filled with war. Margaret knew about war. She had studied it in school and learned of it in church. The Dakota were waging a war to wipe out all whites in Minnesota. No one would be spared. This felt biblical, like what the Israelites of Egypt were subjected to, or the Crusades. The Dakota hoped to regain their land, to sweep the whites away. But how realistic was that?

This, Margaret realized, was a holy war to the Dakota. But neither the Americans nor their government would see it that way. How could the Dakota even think it would work? There were many Dakota. But there were so many whites. But then, Margaret chided herself, the ones who had started this were not thinking. Brown Wing was like Jakob. He would not listen. He jumped into things without thinking. His way was right, even though no one else would agree. Disagreement only forced him to become more entrenched in his belief.

Both Brown Wing and Jakob were hot tempered. They often got into fights over the smallest of issues. Jakob and Brown Wing had once played together. Margaret could remember their competitions—who could catch the most fish, climb the highest tree, and pick the most berries. Leap the farthest. Always without thinking. Winona had chuckled with Margaret about it. Their fathers said they were just boys, but Brown Wing and Jakob never seemed to grow out of their willful behaviors. They just seemed to get worse, soon not able to see each other without anger coming between them. Both were so angry, all the time, at everything.

Jakob had been so mad at not joining the War Between the States. He was too young. Still young boys joined. They pretended to be older, and some got in. Like most boys his age, Jakob was excited about fighting. He didn't think about the why, just about the fight.

Margaret leaned over to whisper her thoughts of Jakob to Winona, when a soft snore escaped her friend's lips. Margaret knew her friend could use a nap. She had run all night to warn them. Margaret didn't think she herself would have had the strength to do that. Winona had always been stronger and faster and better at everything.

Margaret let her mind drift to the first time she'd met Winona. It seemed like they had been friends since that first meeting outside the Episcopal Church on the Lower Agency. It was the church Chief Taoyateduta went to, Winona told her as way of greeting. At that point, Margaret had not even known who Taoyateduta was, later she learned that many whites called him Little Crow. But Margaret could tell that he was important, and she felt her eyes widen in awe.

Margaret's father had been one of the first to move into the new land opened north of the Minnesota River Valley. Valley land was richer than their old farmland. Margaret learned later that it was newly opened Dakota land. More importantly, she learned that newly opened to her father, meant newly taken to the Dakota.

Of course, none of that had been discussed between the girls when they first met. Those stories came later during long summer days spent berry picking, gathering flowers, climbing trees. They had started sharing small stories, and, learning that their stories did not travel back to their mothers and fathers, they spoke more openly to each other. They shared dreams and hopes as well as their frustrations with hardheaded brothers and stubborn fathers. If only she could go back to those endless days!

A sharp crack, followed by two more, interrupted her pleas-
ant thoughts. Winona woke up. From the look on each other's
faces, Winona and Margaret knew there was no mistaking what
each of them had heard: Gunshots.

Chapter 5

The War Party Arrives

WINONA JERKED AWAKE. How could she have fallen asleep at a time like this? Her heart was pounding. Had there been three shots or four? She looked at Margaret. Margaret help up four fingers. Winona pressed the ground with her hand. Margaret understood and lay down, trying to make herself as small as possible. Margaret reached her hand out and helped her mother to realize she needed to lie still as well.

Their eyes were all wide in shock. Winona wanted to look, but knew she didn't dare. A war party would scan the prairie trying to find the family that had left. She felt through her skirt for her knife. Holding it calmed her some. The shots seemed a way off, but as she had been asleep, she could not be sure.

Looking to Margaret she mouthed, "Close or far?"

Margaret shook her head. She did not know, could not tell.

"Loud!" Margaret whispered. "Very loud!"

"Loud means they are close." Winona whispered. "We'll stay down. Safer to stay hidden." Margaret nodded, as did her Mother. Isaac seemed asleep in his blanket. Winona hoped he would stay asleep and quiet.

Winona strained her ears, but she could hear nothing. She pressed one ear to the ground, distant thuds came to her, perhaps horses. *What was going on? Can I risk looking? It's so quiet.*

"Listen." Margaret whispered.

"I don't hear anything." Winona hissed back.

"That's what I mean. The chickens should be squawking. Or the cows . . . or something. There's no noise. I've never heard the farm this quiet. No birds? Nothing. Shouldn't there be some noise?"

Winona's eyes widened. The entire farm was holding its breath, just like they were. She could not hazard a look. Who knew where the war party was. Dakota warriors were the best at moving silent. Even through dry prairie grass. They'd sense her movement before she could see them. As agonizing as it was to keep still, she had to.

"Stay still. Keep quiet," Winona whispered.

Both Margaret and her Mother nodded. Winona fingered the handle of her knife and listened with every part of her body. She could see Margaret's lips moving and knew she was praying even though she couldn't hear the words.

Thinking a prayer couldn't hurt, Winona spoke to Wakantanka, the Great Spirit. *Please let us live, please! Please let us get out if this. Please. Guide us, what should we do? Is it better to stay still? Should I try to see what is happening? Guide us, please!* Repeating the words over and over comforted her. Perhaps the Great Spirit would send her a sign. Something that would help their next decision come a little easier.

Suddenly she heard noise. The braves were approaching the house. They were careless and loud. Moving and talking, she could almost see them, their noise was so loud. It sounded as if there were four. She raised four fingers to Margaret, who nodded her understanding. By moving so loudly, the braves believed no one to be near. That was good, Winona thought. They won't be scanning the prairie. She could try to peer over the tall grass, if she moved slowly enough. A sudden movement would make even the most careless brave see her.

Winona motioned to Margaret to stay down but started inching herself upwards.

The braves were loudly discussing how easy this was. It was not Brown Wing, Winona could tell by their voices. She wasn't sure they were from Red Middle Voice's band. They did not sound familiar. They were convinced a victory was theirs. One of the braves was loudly showing off his gun to the others. He bragged about how easy it had been to kill the white boy and that he would kill many more now with this gun. One of the others joked and said, "Or chickens," and they all laughed. Winona was extremely grateful that Margaret knew so little of the Dakota language.

Moving very slowly, Winona crouched on her heels. Slowly she eased herself up. Her head was level with the grass, but she could not see through the prairie. She would be visible, if she went higher. Instead she crouched back down and eased herself behind the tree. Slowly she edged herself higher above the grass line but behind the tree. The tree bark matched her dark hair. At least she hoped so. Easing her head around and angling her neck she dared to show her forehead and one eye.

There were four. She was right. All were dressed in leggings. Paint decorated their chests and two had feathers tied in their hair. They had dismounted and dropped the reins. They were all headed into the house. Not leaving one warrior behind for the horses or to watch for enemies. They not only felt safe, but were acting stupid as well. Winona chided them in her head. She could almost hear her father lecturing them to always leave the youngest by the horses. A warrior without a horse was a dead warrior.

Soon noises reached their ears. The sounds of destruction, crockery smashing, wood breaking. *Do they have to destroy everything?* Winona thought. They came back out. One of the warriors paused to peer over the prairie. Winona resisted the urge to duck back behind the tree. He was more likely to see the movement than her face. He did not look long, before following the other three. Arguing loudly, all went from the house to the barn. Arguing about whether to burn the house and barn or not, if they would find horses, what they should take, where the rest of the family had gone. One brave said, "Who cares as long as they're gone!"

Three of the braves went into the barn. The fourth, Winona named him Watcher. He looked around him. His back was to her. She felt it was safe to keep watching. One of the older braves came out, leading the cow. "Horses are all gone, they must have rode away, when they heard us coming!" They laughed at that.

They think they are so tough! Winona thought, but why are they here when Taoyateduta asked for all braves to attack together. They are not as brave as they would like to think they are. The brave she called, Watcher, mounted his horse and told the others to come. Two ran back into the house, the noise of metal crashing reached Winona's ears. "It'll burn now!" they shouted as they ran back out and mounted their horses. Winona thought one of the horses looked as if it was the farm horse. The brave riding it was the youngest by far. He might have been riding behind one of the others before they found Jakob and his horse.

Winona started to stand, but thought better of it just in time. Watcher spun his horse around and seemed to be riding straight for her. Winona fought against her instinct to run. She froze and tried to stay as still as possible. His horse thundered towards her, devouring the prairie between them. Just when Winona was convinced he would be upon her, he turned back and galloped to the head of the line. The four followed the farm's trail back to the main road. Winona could feel the bile taste of panic in her mouth. She had almost spooked like a bird, flushed herself out of the prairie. The braves would have killed her friends and taken Winona back in disgrace.

Slowly, Winona sank to the ground. *It is all a game to them,* Winona thought. Turning to Margaret she whispered, "They are boys playing at war. Hate and destruction has filled their hearts. They should be with the others attacking Fort Ridgley. Where there is one band, there will be more. The house is burning. The fire will draw attention. We need to leave. Now! Quickly, help your mother and Isaac. I'll fetch some necessaries!"

Margaret watched Winona run towards the house; she was bent over but moving fast. Margaret wondered if Jakob had fired on the Dakota, or if the shots had been aimed at someone else. She helped her mother stand, and hoped that Jakob was far away. He had been so ready for war.

Jakob had begged their father every night to let him fight in the War Between the States. Pa wouldn't hear of it. Margaret and Jakob had heard of boys as young as sixteen enlisting but they both didn't think Jakob could stand on eighteen convincingly enough. He was too thin and short with a flop of hair that always fell into his eyes making him look even younger.

Margaret tried to figure out how long ago Jakob had left. She felt he could have been close to the ferry by now, if he had headed to the agency on the reservation. But she didn't know where he was going. *Besides towards a fight!* She thought and mentally shushed herself. Margaret wanted no real harm to come to him. She had never been able to reason with him, even when he wasn't angry. He was as hardheaded as their father. Both of them riding out to do justice on the Dakota troublemakers.

Winona had reached the clothesline. She grabbed the nappies, an apron and some dishtowels that were drying in the warm sun. Good thinking, Margaret thought and then turned to assist her mother. Ma seemed dazed and confused. Margaret bent and lifted Isaac from where he was sleeping on the grass. She thought her mother didn't look up to carrying the baby. Margaret felt like something very large had shifted in her universe. She and Winona seemed to be in charge. It felt odd. Margaret felt unbalanced, like the earth was tipping. Clutching baby Isaac to her, she reached for her mother's hand. Perhaps holding on would help her balance.

Winona came back. She put the clothing from the line down. Using Margaret's shawl, Winona wrapped the babe Isaac in it. She tied the ends around Margaret's back. "I wish we had a cradleboard. But this will help keep Isaac secure and your hands free to carry something, or help your mother."

Before picking up the breakfast bundle, Margaret took a long drink of the still warm milk. It was difficult to drink from the milk pail with Isaac between her and the bucket. Winona chuckled at her, then drank some when it was offered. She made a face though. Winona hated milk. Margaret made her mother take a drink and then dumped the little that was left. It seemed impractical to carry such a small amount. Plus it would sour if left in the sun any longer. She wiped the pail out with her apron, and then put the clean nappies, extra apron and the dishtowels in. She put the breakfast bundle on the top.

"Well, I guess we are all packed up. Which way do we go?"

"To the creek. We need water and a place to hide while the sun is high." Winona answered. "But wait." She took out her knife and started to dig in the earth under the tree. She cut a piece of sod away, then used her hands to pull out the dry crumbly earth underneath. After a few handfuls she pulled out a leather bundle. "Our treasures," Winona said and, carrying the bundle, strode towards the creek. Her back to the farm and holding Mother's hand, Margaret followed.

"My bonnet! We need our bonnets! Margaret, run and fetch them from the porch, we cannot be out in the sun without them." Margaret's mother blurted. Margaret stopped and turned her hand using it to guide her mother's eyes back to the farmhouse. It was in flames, higher than Margaret thought flames could go.

"We will have to make do without them, Ma. It'll be all right. No one we meet today will be that concerned about whether we have a few more freckles than usual."

Winona chuckled at Margaret's words. "I always thought you wore more clothes than were good for you. Petticoats, hoop skirts, under skirts, top skirts, kerchiefs, aprons, shawls, wraps, bonnets and hats. How much cloth does it take to clothe one of you anyway?"

Margaret laughed but noticing that mother's eyes got impossibly wide. She indicated to Winona with her eyes that less said might be best. Winona nodded back and continued to lead the way. Margaret took one last look at everything she owned going up in smoke, and followed Winona. Gently she squeezed her mother's hand and was reassured when mother squeezed back.

Chapter 6

On the Move

Winona skirted the barn and outhouse. She walked quickly. Staying close to the wheel tracks that led to the road. She did not walk in the open. The cornfield provided the feeling of shelter as they walked between the rows. Without speaking, she and Margaret had decided to avoid the roads and keep in the grass and fields for as much of the journey as possible. She motioned for Margaret to continue in the direction they were going and whispered that she'd catch up.

"Jakob?" Margaret questioned her. Winona nodded and strode away quickly before Margaret decided to come with her.

She walked back the way they had come and then ran through the farmyard. The heat from the house fire hurt her face she was so close. She ran quickly to the trail leading to the main road. Running along it, Winona was nervous to be in the open. Hopefully, she would hear or sense the horses of another war party before they would see her. She ran in the open for what felt like a very long time.

Then she saw him. Jakob. He lay in the open. His head was facing the sky. His eyes were open.

Winona watched him for a long time, willing him to get up or make some movement. She moved closer and saw what she had suspected. Jakob was not going to get up ever again. She tried to close his eyes. But they would not shut. Winona knew Jakob was an ornery boy. But he did not deserve to die. Why did this have to happen? Why couldn't the young Dakota listen to the elders? Winona thought of her brother, his friends, the four braves with anger. How did they think killing was going to solve any of their problems? Chief Taoyat-eduta had said they would all die. Still they voted for war? Why not try one more time to get their food? Why not try to go to Washington and speak with the Great White Father? If the the traders would stop their cheating all would be better. Surely, the Great White Father Lin-coln would listen to the Dakota's pleas.

But the gold was late. Now it was too late to stop this war. I have to get Margaret to safety. That is all I can do now.

She wondered about the greed of some white men as she walked back into the cornfield. She would use the prairie or the cornfields to hide her as she walked back. Winona wondered if the gold was late because the Great White Father had run out of money, like it was said. The War between the States was costing a lot—both in gold and in men. Or was it late because of the trader's greed? What if they were keeping it from the Dakota to drive harder bargains. Many white men had too much greed. They lived only to gain more. Their greed allowed children to go hungry so they could have more gold in their pockets. It was their fault this war. No one would see it that way. But it was true.

Winona knew that not all whites were like this but the greed and anger of the few had made life unbearable for all of the Dakota. Now the Dakota felt they had no choice. Too many would die. But not, she resolved, as she walked quietly back to her friend and what was left of her friend's family, us.

Margaret gasped in fright when Winona came up beside her and took her hand. She had not heard her walking up to them. She checked to make sure her Mother was all right but noticed that her Mother's eyes were vacant and a bit glazed. She wasn't sure if her mother had even noticed that Winona had left and now returned.

Margaret looked at Winona with a hopeful expression. Perhaps Jakob had made it away from the war party. Winona shook her head and mouthed, "Er ist tot." Winona knew more English than German but she used both without noticing.

Margaret stumbled and then found the resolve to continue. Perhaps if Jakob had listened to her, he'd still be alive. He'd be with them. But he never had listened before, and now he never would again. She had to be strong for her Mother, the baby, and for Winona. It's just us, she reminded herself. We have to be strong for each other. Winona squeezed her hand to reassure her and then let go to walk in the lead. Side by side walking was difficult in the long grass.

After walking all morning, they finally reached Beaver Creek. Finding a tree, Winona helped Margaret sit down under it and untied baby Isaac. Isaac was grizzling and Margaret's mother reached out her arms for him. Winona went to the creek and drank her fill. Then she told Margaret to go. Margaret returned to find her mother using the tree trunk to support her back while she nursed Isaac.

Margaret unpacked the clean clothes, and the breakfast bundle. She then fetched a bucket of water for her mother to drink when she was done nursing. Her neck and shoulders hurt, as did the small of her back. A baby sure didn't look like much, but Isaac weighed a lot. She hoped her mother or Winona would take a turn carrying him next.

Margaret sat with Winona a little ways off from Mother and the nursing Isaac. Speaking softly, so as not to be heard, Margaret asked, "Should we try to get to the Redwood Ferry?" The ferry would take them to the Indian agency and the Reverend Hinman's missionary. "That should be safe."

"I'm not sure it will be safe. I told you that this morning. Chief Taoyateduta ordered attacks for the agency and the fort. The agency has no cannon. Only the fort does. I think we should try to get to the fort. There are soldiers there to protect you."

"But, churches are always safe in war," hissed Margaret. "The Dakota could take the fort. There are so few soldiers there. So many left yesterday to join the War in the South."

"They'll be sent for. Your soldier captains will send riders to bring them back. The soldiers will be stronger than the agents. We must get to the fort. We can get there if we can walk all day. Then I can sneak us close after nightfall." Winona stubbornly insisted on her original plan. She knew the cannon could not be overtaken. Plus the buildings were stone. They would give protection.

"You never listen to me!" Margaret was losing her temper. "We can't possibly reach Fort Ridgley tonight. Mother walks too slowly. The Dakota are mad at the agents and traders. They'll die at Dakota hands. However, the Dakota won't attack the chapel. The reverend will keep us safe. He'll have a plan for us!"

"Think of Jakob, Margaret. He was an annoying boy. But he did no wrong to any Dakota. He was killed. Why would my brother in his anger, honor your God? He will not. The other warriors are like him. They are out of control. This is like a fire. It will burn everyone near it. We must stay out of sight, walk as quickly as we can. But we must make for the big guns and the soldiers. That is our only hope."

"I agree." Mother's voice interrupted their argument. She was setting out the biscuits and cooked ham. "We should eat our fill. This meat will spoil in the hot sun. Then we should drink our fill and head as fast as we can to the fort. Thank you, Winona, for saving us. We'll follow you. Wherever you think we should go."

Winona nodded her agreement, while Margaret huffed and puffed her anger away.

45

After nibbling all of the biscuits, they each drank from the stream. Mother changed Isaac's nappy and Margaret rinsed it out in the stream. She placed it on top of their bucket of possessions. It would dry and bleach in the sun. She sat down and took off her stockings and shoes. Her mother followed her example. Winona removed her leggings and moccasins. Then all three waded through the creek. Mother carried Isaac, who napped peacefully in her arms. They paused at the top of the opposite bank. Underneath another tree, they sat and replaced their footwear. Winona spent some time looking over the prairie in every direction. Finally, she motioned to Margaret and her mother to follow. Thankfully, Mother carried the baby. Margaret tied the shawl around her to help support him. Then, single file, they started to walk again.

Winona felt that it was worse after the break than before. Her feet, her legs, and her head all ached. She was used to walking and working all day—why was she in pain now, she wondered, surprised. Perhaps it was because her body and mind were fighting. Her body wanted to run, yet her mind resisted the insane pull to just run. Her body felt that if she ran fast enough, she would surely outrun everything, the war, the killing, and the haunted look in Margaret's eyes.

She had not told Margaret this but any Dakota who had friends with the whites were to be killed as well. The half-breeds, those who were part Dakota and part white. They were to be killed too. Her brother hated that Winona had a white friend. Yet, he had found her eyes while the chiefs discussed who would be attacked. Brown Wing usually looked at Winona with mischief or anger in his eyes. This time his eyes had a strong message: "Run, save her!" they said.

Winona knew he was offering her a promise not to come after her friend. There was no such guarantee from any of the other warriors. As she had seen this morning at the farm. Her fear for Margaret had propelled her to sneak away from the council. Once free of all their eyes, she had run as fast as she could. It had felt so good to run. To feel in charge of her body. She had so little power but she could run. She ran faster than she had ever run before. It felt like the prairie itself was urging her on. *Run. Run before it is too late*, the grasses whispered to her.

Winona could feel her blood pumping fast again, her heart and her body wanted her to run again. But Winona forced her heart to slow. She needed to stay calm. She might be able to outrun the danger, but her friends could not. She had to get them to safety, and then she could run as fast as she could to rejoin her tribe. Winona rubbed her jaw, her temple too. She could not outrun a bullet. Better to hide so the bullet was never fired.

Moving ahead of Margaret she came to a wagon trail. She motioned for Margaret to cross and keep moving in their same direction while she moved beside the trail staying in the longer grass, and later the corn that was planted in neat rows beside it.

She reached a farmstead but did not venture too close. It all looked quiet, as if the farmer and his family had simply gone into town for the day, but Winona did not think it was as peaceful as it looked. Carefully skirting around, using the corn and then the orderly garden as cover, she approached the lean-to at the back of the cabin. Whistling a Killdeer's call. She waited. If there were any Dakota hiding she knew they would whistle a greeting back to her. Only silence. Gathering her courage, she ran the last few steps in the open and burst through the door.

She immediately wished she hadn't. The family had all been killed at breakfast. Two extra plates had been set. The plates still held food. Winona figured the braves had been invited to eat with the family. So many of the settlers did this, knowing how hungry the Dakota were. This family had its kindness repaid with death.

Winona was sickened by what she saw, but knew that she needed to bring food to the others. They needed food to keep going. She grabbed a towel from the dry sink and wrapped up the remaining biscuits sitting on the platter. She put the bits of pork left in the pan on the stove into her towel as well. She could not bring herself to touch the food left on the plates. Then she ran out of the cabin, caring not if she was seen or heard but simply desiring to put as much distance from herself and the kitchen of death as she could.

Chapter 7

A Storm Brews

Margaret could see that Winona was scared. Her eyes were white-rimmed and darting around in her head. She carried a small bundle and seemed frightened beyond belief. Margaret reached for her hand and understood that she wished not to talk, so for a while they simply walked hand in hand in front of her mother. Finally, she felt Winona's body relax. Just as she was about to ask what happened, Mother fell to her knees.

Margaret turned around and started to help her stand. Before she could get her to her feet, they all heard voices. The voices spoke in Dakota. All were male. Margaret sank to her knees beside her mother, and then lay down pulling mother down as well. She held her breath. How close had they come to stumbling into their deaths?

Margaret let her breath out very slowly and glanced at Winona. Winona gestured that the Dakota were in front of them and then gave a small, wry smile. *Why would that be worth a smile,* Margaret wondered. *What does it matter if they're in front? Or behind?* So what if they were right beside? If they were close enough to hear them that was too close for comfort.

After the conversation and noise of the braves had passed, Margaret continued to stay down. Her mother also seemed content to stay hidden. Her mother shifted her position slightly to nurse Isaac. Margaret was impressed with how well her mother was adapting to hiding, and keeping Isaac quiet.

Rolling to her side, she whispered to Winona. "Why are you smiling?"

Winona cut her eyes behind them and then ahead of them. Margaret followed with her own eyes, not understanding at first. Then she did. The grass behind them was flattened, crushed by their feet as they walked through the prairie. If the war party had come from behind, it would have followed their path straight to them.

"From now on," Winona whispered, "I will walk ahead and you will pull the grass up behind us to disguise out path. We were lucky once. But that kind of stupidity will cost us our lives!"

Winona scolded herself for being such a fool. She was leaving a trail like a Mato, a bear. Any idiot could follow the path they had left. Margaret was muttering to herself as she pulled the grass up behind them. Winona thought she heard her say *dummkopf*. A word usually reserved for Jakob. She allowed herself a smile, as she continued to walk carefully through the long grass.

She now hoped to get them to Birch Coulee Creek before nightfall. As much as she would hate to admit it, she would have to tell Margaret she had been right. They could not possibly cover the distance to the fort in one day. They moved at the pace of a snail. Margaret's mother slowed them down immensely. But Margaret only had her mother and baby Isaac left. It was better to go slow and to stay alive. Now though they would go even slower, as Margaret concealed their path.

Winona was terribly thirsty. It had been a long time since they last had a drink. She had allowed them to rest and eat what she had found earlier. It was not a lot of food. However, Winona was much more thirsty than hungry. Still, she knew they needed to get more food. They would be hungry tonight after they drank from the creek.

If I found another farmstead, we could use the well. I'd have to make sure there weren't any bodies first. I don't know if Mar-

garet or her mother would be able to see their neighbors dead and mutilated. Perhaps it would be better if I got them to the creek and hidden. I could go scout for supplies after.

This made the most sense to Winona, and she picked up her pace. But she was quickly forced to slow down as Margaret's mother was unable to walk any faster. Both Margaret and her mother had pink faces now. Whether from exertion or the hot sun, Winona did not know. It was very hot. The sun was directly overhead. The grass crackled under their feet. Winona knew she should slow down even more so they would be quieter, but she could not. It was torture to hear all the noise they made. Particularly knowing that Margaret thought she was being quiet.

Hopefully, the war parties would be making more noise than they were. The last two certainly had. Men who are brave make more noise, Winona hoped, than women who are trying to hide.

Winona noticed the weather was changing. Rapidly. The wind picked up strength and shifted from the east to blowing from the west. Clouds hid the sun, and darker storm clouds were building in the west. This was a blessing. The heat would drop. But as Winona glanced at the gathering storm clouds, she realized it was a large storm coming. They would need some sort of shelter.

The creek would have trees. A collection of them was good to keep the rain off. A tree by itself would attract lightening. Winona could see some trees to her right. That meant the creek was close, it would have trees overhanging the water. She told the group to hurry. "We need to get to those trees and out of this storm."

Margaret's mother walked more quickly to keep up. But Margaret herself continued to curse under her breath and dawdle behind trying to get the grass to stand up, covering their trail. Winona dashed back and pointed to the clouds.

"The rain will flatten all of it, hiding our trail. We need to hurry and get out of it before it opens up." Running to the front again, she passed Margaret's mother. Just as she suspected, white ladies could not run, but she was walking faster than she had all day. Winona motioned to her to stop and untied Isaac. Running ahead with him, she hoped to get him under the trees and out of the storm. This had come up fast. There might be hail, but most certainly the rain would be cold.

When she got close to the trees, Winona saw there was a creek. Very small, too small to be the Birch Coulee but large enough to have fresh water. Plus she found a pretty good hiding spot underneath the willows growing by the creek's bank. Winona laid Isaac down under the willow. Then she went and drank. As always, when she was so thirsty, Winona could not believe how good the water tasted.

The heat was still stifling, so Winona scooped water to her neck and face. Margaret joined her at the water's edge. After drinking her fill, she also splashed her face and neck. The girls looked at each other and grinned. Sometimes they could forget what they were running away from.

Winona went back to where she had dropped the bucket. She pulled out the cloths, and fetched some water for Margaret's mother. Margaret helped get her mother settled against the tree trunk, and then placed Isaac in her arms.

"Wait here with your mother," Winona said. "Try to stay as quiet as possible. I'm going to try to find us something to eat." Winona rushed away. She did not mind getting caught in the rain. Now that her thirst was quenched, she realized she was famished, and she hoped to find a farmstead close by. The creek would not have any fish big enough for supper, even if she could suddenly develop the skill to catch one. No it was best to raid a farmhouse.

She backtracked along their path to the creek. Margaret had done a good job. A skilled warrior might read their tracks but the war parties they had seen today were too young and moving too fast to see their path now that it was less obvious. She hoped it would pour, pushing the grass down and effectively covering their tracks.

Her hair felt as if it was standing on end, the lightening would come very soon. She could hear the thunder rolling over the prairie. Finding a small rise, she stared at the storm as it came closer. Peering carefully in all directions, She could see a small house and outbuildings not far away. As much as she did not wish to see any more death or destruction, she knew they needed something to eat to continue. She stepped back to tell Margaret but then thought better of it. Margaret was stubborn and mule headed. She would insist on coming along. If there were braves waiting at the farmstead, Winona had a much better chance talking her way out of trouble by herself.

She ran quickly. She was by herself. If they were warriors, they would believe her story of following them to get something to eat. The farm seemed deserted. There were no birds calling, no noise from the barn either. Animals often got quiet before a storm but there was usually still some rustling in the straw as they shifted position. This place was eerily quiet just as the last farmstead had been. Winona paused at the cornfield. She was trying to get up her nerve to go inside, when she noticed a small door on the side of a small hill. Just a grassy hill, with a door in it. Winona had noticed these before. Margaret had one. A root cellar, she had called it.

There might be food in there and Winona would not have to go in the house. It was too early and too hot for them to have done any butchering. But there might be some jars canned from last season.

Slowly she eased her way in and waited for her eyes to adjust. There wasn't much. There were some jars, two of them, it really did not matter to Winona what was in the jars. It was food. She also found some small potatoes and onions in a tin pan. *Probably meant for tonight's supper,* Winona thought. There was a burlap bag on a hook by the door, she wrapped the jars in the burlap and placed them in the pan with the onions and potatoes. They would not make much noise this way.

She turned around, ready to leave, when she caught a shadow hanging in the back. Could it be? It was! A chunk of pork, ham as Margaret called it. This was one of Winona's favorite things to eat. Delighted, she tucked it under her arm and slowly pulled the door shut.

Carefully she looked around her surroundings and then darted quickly back to the cornfield. She looked behind her to see if she had left many tracks. She didn't see any. She turned to run back to their hiding spot when the rain started. Happily, Winona ran though the pelting drops. It was a nice heavy rain. It would wipe away all traces of their path. Smiling and awkwardly running as fast as she could, carrying the tin and the ham. Winona could picture the looks of delight on Margaret and her mother's faces!

Chapter 8

A Feast

MARGARET COULD NOT BELIEVE HER EYES. Winona had brought back a feast. They could eat until their bellies bulged and still have plenty for tomorrow. Margaret had worried about Winona as the rain had started before Winona made it back to their hiding spot. The clouds had really opened up, and the rain fell by the bucketful. Lightening zigzagged the sky and the thunder was so close it made their hearts jump.

"Let's start a fire. Go get some dry wood from under the trees. I'll get it started." Margaret ran off to gather as many dry branches as she could. Winona found a dry spot under the tree. She piled some small twigs and small branches together. Making a teepee shape. In the middle she piled dry leaves and grasses to catch a spark quickly. Winona pulled out her fire starter kit from her bag, striking the flint and steel together until sparks flew into the dry tinder.

By the time Margaret returned with her second armful of branches, the fire was cozily crackling. Winona went to the creek and found a flat rock. She used a stick to smooth out the fire, shaping the new branches into a ring. Setting the rock in the middle of the fire, she continued to feed the fire all around the rock, keeping it blazing happily.

Pulling out her knife, she used it to cut the potatoes, onion and ham into slices. She placed these in the tin pan and put it on the rock in the middle of the fire. "We'll need more wood." Margaret ran to gather more. Winona tended the fire and turned the potatoes and ham over with her knife. The potatoes and onion sizzled in the fat from the ham. It smelled heavenly, when Margaret returned with her fourth load of wood.

Margaret happily ignored the fact that the potatoes and onions had not been washed first. Her Mother did not notice. One of the jars held beets. They ate all of them, cold and pickled right from the jar, while they waited for their feast to finish cooking. Winona sharpened a stick for each of them and these they used to spear their supper straight from the pan.

"I've never eaten better." Margaret's mother exclaimed. She laid out her shawl and lay down close to the fire and used Margaret's shawl to wrap Isaac close to her. "We should sleep. Let the fire die down, we can tend it in the morning."

Her Mother fell asleep quickly, and Margaret tried to follow. But her entire body ached. She knew she should be happy they were alive instead of whimpering about wanting a bed. But still, she felt terribly uncomfortable. Winona had started a new batch to of potatoes and ham to cook. "They'll be easier to eat in the morning. After the fire has died down, cover the food with a towel or apron."

"Why can't you cover it? Won't you be here? Where are you going?" Margaret questioned her friend.

"I need to get back to my village. Or to Taoyateduta's village. His is closer. There may be more warriors gathered at his fire tonight. I can be there and back before daybreak. I know you do not want me to leave but information will help us all stay safe and alive. This is a good hiding spot. Stay here, rest and eat. I'll be back. I promise. Do not be stubborn or foolish. Do not try to go on without me. I will come back."

"Don't go. We don't need information that badly. Your plan is good. Stay here. We should stay together," Margaret begged.

"It will be fine. Please, stay here. Do not try to leave without me. I will be back by the sunrise. The rain means the warriors will have abandoned all their attacks. They will not fight in the rain. It will be safe until tomorrow morning. Isaac is fine. You have food and water. Rest, we will need your strength to get your mother moving in the morning." Winona kissed her cheek and was gone.

Margaret did not want her to leave. She felt safer with her friend close by. What would happen if the babe cried, if their hiding spot was found, if a war party found them? All of her thoughts whirled around in her brain. They refused to go away and her anxiety over these thoughts would not allow her to sleep. She spread an apron next to the flickering fire. Lying down, she watched the flames. She fed the fire until she worried someone would see it, and then she let it die into embers.

She knew that Winona was right. Little Crow would be making his plans. Winona needed to hear them. If she knew where the next attacks would be, they would be safer. She had to go. But, Margaret thought, *She didn't have to look like she would enjoy leaving so much.*

Chapter 9

Running Again

WINONA RAN AS QUIETLY AS SHE COULD, it felt so good to run. Her body had been pushed beyond anything she had ever done before. But as always, once she started running, she felt better. Following the creek, she came to the Minnesota River, the one the whites had called St. Peter for so long. It was deep here, but Winona was a strong swimmer. Her mother had taught her when she was young. It was a skill every Dakota should have, she'd said. Taking off her clothes, knife and bag. She bundled them on top of her head. The rain had stopped some time ago. It would be better to put dry clothes on a wet body, then to be in wet clothes all night.

It took Winona longer than it usually did to swim across. Swimming one handed slowed her down as did the rain-swollen current. *Perhaps*, she had to admit to herself, *I might be a little overtired. I have not slept and am pushing myself too hard. Father says even a warrior must stop to rest if he is to stay strong.*

Stumbling ashore on the other side, Winona rested in the wet grass. Then she dressed. She hated the feeling of her leggings going over her wet legs, her short gown stuck to her wet back. But this could not be helped. She had to move fast, anyone she might see would think she had gotten caught in the rain. She made her way slowly to where she thought Taoyateduta's village should be. She was not too far off, and adjusted her pace as she heard the yells and whistles of the braves triumphantly bragging of their attacks.

They spoke loudly and held high their plunder. Everywhere she looked she could see braves, drying and warming themselves by their fires. Telling their families of their victories. There were far more people here than usually were in Taoyateduta's village. Winona supposed many had gathered here for the same reason she had. To hear what today had brought and learn of tomorrow's plan.

Winona kept to the outskirts of the teepees and fires, trying to not be noticed. She did not want to explain her absence to anyone. Someone might guess she was helping her German friend. She crept slowly till she could see Taoyateduta's tall two-story house.

As she edged closer, she realized something. She had not noticed it at first. There were many mixed bloods and whites here. Most of the whites were women and children and they were filthy. Many wore a terrified expression. Most were huddled in groups or working under the supervision of Dakota women. Winona knew they were prisoners, taken to be used for trade with the whites after the fighting was over. She felt both horrified and grateful to see so many. She was grateful many children and women had been saved, but horrified thinking of how many men must have died. These women and children were without fathers and husbands. The violence had spread very far in just one day. She and Margaret were lucky to have been spared, very lucky indeed.

As if on cue, the warriors started gathering close to Taoyateduta's fire. The blaze was large like a council fire should be, so all could see and be heard. This was not what Winona wanted. She wanted to see and hear but not to be seen. She willed herself to be unnoticed and stayed in the shadows. The braves settled themselves by the fire. Their chiefs sat in front. Their war bonnets cast long shadows. Winona searched for her father. He took such pride in his war feathers and paint. But she could not find him. As the young braves gathered behind their chiefs, she realized he was not there.

Why would he not be here? No one from her tribe was. She looked at all the young men, but could not find her brother anywhere either. Perhaps they were farther out and would return later. Winona listened to the silence of the chiefs and the excited voices of the young men.

The young men were boasting. They told others and themselves how brave they were, how many eagle feathers they would be awarded. They boasted of the congratulations their chiefs and elders would bestow on them. They boasted how they would tell these stories to their children's children right here at this very place for the Dakota would now have this land forever as the battles would drive the whites away, and they would have forced the whites to move or die.

Their boasting did not last long. Chief Taoyateduta did not shower them with praise. Instead he scolded them, shamed them as if they were young boys who had run off to play. "Killing the farmers will not win this war. You will not drive away white men by killing them when they are unarmed. Killing women and children will not give us victory. Warriors do not kill those who are not they themselves warriors. Do we kill unarmed Ojibways? We do not. We attack armed men. We attack warriors. My braves, you fought like children today. You were undisciplined and foolish. We have but a few days before the entire American Army arrives. We must stand together and take the fort. It is the way to fight a war with honor. I am ashamed of you.

"You ought not to kill women and children. Wakantanka, the Great Spirit will reproach you for it in the afterlife. This will make you weak in battle. You were too hasty in spreading out into the farmland. I know you wish this land to be yours again. But you are doing wrong if you fight this way. You should have killed only those who have been robbing us so long. Hereafter, make war after the manner of the white man. Kill soldiers. Kill those who are armed. We fight together or we will die alone."

He paused and let his words sink in. Winona could hear murmurs of anger and dissent. But no one dared speak. The war parties had been acting without orders. Winona had suspected this was true. Now she knew it. Taoyateduta spoke again.

"I will meet with the council. Go away warriors. Go in shame. You will be needed in the morning to restore honor to yourselves and to all Dakota. You must join together to fight the soldiers at Fort Ridgley in the morning. The news of your attacks on helpless men, women and children is spreading as fast as a horse can run. Soon soldiers will be sent from Fort Snelling. They will come to attack all Dakota. We have to attack as one tomorrow and will only achieve victory if we work together, fight together. Do not break off into small bands to thieve, plunder and murder the farmers. Now go away. I am ashamed of you. Come to me tomorrow as men, not troublesome boys."

That broke up the crowd quickly. The braves wandered, defeated, back to their cooking fires. They whispered to themselves that perhaps Little Crow was right. After all, they needed to defeat the soldiers. They had gotten carried away, that was all. For many it had been their first battle. They were untrained, they said to themselves. Now they knew what they must do. Tomorrow they would follow Chief Taoyateduta.

Many voiced that it could not be much harder to kill soldiers than killing farmers. Whites were not trained from childhood to be warriors like Dakota men were. So the whites, soldiers they may be in name, would not be the warriors they were, not in heart or spirit.

Winona continued to search through the crowd, although there were many warriors from all of the bands she knew, she still had not seen any from her own band. Red Middle Voice's warriors were conspicuously absent. She could not find her mother's teepee or any of her family. She wondered where they were and whether they were doing something Taoyateduta would approve. Were they still looting farms?

At least Winona did not have to worry about being recognized. But she had hoped to at least see her family. She now had no way of joining them. Her band would have moved after sending the warriors off in the morning. Her mother would have loaded her teepee poles and bundled the skin covering together. Winona sighed. She could go to her village and follow the trail they would have made dragging their teepee poles. But it would take a long time.

She had promised to return to Margaret and her mother, but her own family would have to wait. Feeling she had learned all she could, she turned to head back to the river. As she spun about, she ran right into a warrior. He looked down at her, and Winona gasped. It was Watcher. The older brave from the war party at Margaret's farm. He gazed at her for a long time as if he recognized her. Then he tore his gaze away and continued towards one of the teepees.

Winona's heart was in her throat. She did not stay to see which band he belonged to. She only hoped he thought her gasp was odd, and not that he really remembered her from the prairie. Slowly she walked along the path, working her way quietly back to the river.

Reaching it, she stood slowly. Hoping if someone was following, he or she would make some noise to alert her. Once she was convinced no one was following, she removed her things and bundling them on top of her head swam back to the other side. She let the current take her downstream some. Their hiding spot was further south than she had first realized. She puzzled over all she had learned. If the fort was to be attacked tomorrow, then it no longer made sense to go there. Perhaps they should try for New Ulm. It was far away from the reservation and the fighting.

Winona thought over her decision as she walked back to her friends. Were friends more important than family? Father would disown her for the choice that she had made. Mother might never speak to her again. *But I could not sit by and allow Margaret to be killed. Or taken prisoner. I had to help her. Of course, I thought it would be easier than it's been.* Winona sighed. Nothing ever was all that easy. She felt closer to Margaret than any one in her village. She had escaped her village as often as she could just to wander around or to meet up with Margaret.

She had often invited Margaret to her teepee. Margaret had come, but Winona truly preferred Margaret's home. Margaret's mother always had something delicious cooking. Winona's mother rarely did these last two years. It was more than food though. It was listening to Margaret's mother read to them on the porch. She read books of explorers and adventurers. Winona's favorite was the story of a family who got shipwrecked on an island. They built themselves a house in a tree.

Winona and Margaret had spent weeks playing in trees after that. Perhaps the choice to leave her family for Margaret's had been made years ago. Winona did not wish to marry a brave and continue with the traditional Dakota ways. Nor did she want to become a missionary as a few half-breed girls did. Her choice to save Margaret she thought had been made hastily. She thought she could warn them, get them to a safe spot, then go home. Now, Winona realized just as the braves had realized, each decision led to consequences far greater than one thinks at the time.

Winona made it back to her friends, concerns swirling in her mind, but she laughed out loud when she saw them. She could not help it. Margaret looked so ridiculous.

Chapter 10

A Change in Plans

ARGARET HEARD WINONA LAUGHING but could not see the humor in their situation. The mosquitoes had been merciless. She could not wrap herself in her shawl, because it was around Mother and Isaac. When the buzzing insects would not leave her hands neck and face alone. She had stripped off her petticoat and wrapped her head and arms inside. Her feet she tucked into her dress. She was miserably contorted to protect herself from being bit, and her friend Winona was laughing at her. Why were the mosquitoes not tormenting her?

Peeking angrily out from under her petticoat, she saw why. Winona was smeared in mud. She held out a handful to Margaret and, disgusted, Margaret smeared it on her hands and neck. Then she went to the creek's bank and spread more on her face, ears and other hand. She felt instant relief. The mud cooled the bites she already had and seemed to prevent the mosquitoes from biting her again. She lay down again and watched Winona smooth out her footprints back to the tree. Winona started to tell her of what she had heard and witnessed in Taoyateduta's village.

Margaret listened to how the men had been chastised by Taoyateduta and planned to attack the fort in the morning. She mumbled an, "I told you so." But she could not keep her eyes open. With Winona back and the mosquitoes at bay, she felt safe. Knowing the warriors would not raid more farmsteads also helped.

The Dakota warriors would not hurt her, her mother, or her friend but instead concentrate their fight with the soldiers. She fell asleep with these thoughts and did not awaken until the birds announced the dawn. She was glad to hear them. Somehow it made the events of yesterday fade if the birds were back to their normal routine today. However, that feeling did not last long as she tried to move. Her body was stiff, sore and covered in dried mud. She frowned.

Margaret tried to shake off her bad mood. She knew she should be thankful she was alive. However, she hurt all over. Every inch of her was sore and as she tried to move, her skin cracked. Looking down at herself, she realized she was absolutely filthy. Muttering, Margaret tried to stand up. Other body parts screamed in anger and pain. Muscles she never knew she had, hurt. She opened her mouth to scream, but her mother was terrified, holding a finger to her lips. Margaret froze instantly. Something was wrong.

Margaret looked around. They were alone. Did Winona ever sleep for more than a few minutes? Her mother gestured again to be quiet and stay still. Margaret's grumpiness vanished. Pure panic and fear coursed through her blood. Her mother placed her hand on her shoulder and whispered in her ear. "Be quiet. Be still until Winona returns."

Winona scouted out their position and did not see anyone. She wanted to stay away, far away from the fort and all the war parties heading for it. She still thought their best chance would be keeping on the move. They had to keep moving east and staying out of sight. New Ulm had the most townspeople and would probably be protected by soldiers. This was the only safe spot she could think of. After Taoyateduta's chastisement last night, she did not believe any warriors would attack the town. She believed today they would fight together. Still not seeing her own band at the village last night made her nervous. Her father might have his band attacking the countryside. They would have to be careful.

Silently, Winona made her way back to Margaret and her mother. When she saw how disgruntled Margaret was, Winona laughed again. Her friend was used to a bed and sheets, warm water to wash in. This was agony for her. Margaret glared at her, and Winona laughed again but stopped quickly.

"Come on," Winona said. "Let's get you cleaned up. Its safe, and you will feel a lot better." Winona led Margaret to the creek and helped her wash her face, arms, and legs. She rinsed out her petticoat and laid it on a branch in the early sunshine to dry. Together, they walked back to the embers of last night's fire. Winona poked them until she found a few that glowed. Carefully, she added small twigs and larger branches until it crackled merrily around their cook stone.

Margaret felt her nose, her cheeks and her forehead were all sunburned and they hurt when she touched them. Her mother was right after all—a bonnet was an essential piece of clothing. She was covered in mosquito bites as well, making her sunburn itch and burn even worse.

Winona kept her tongue in check and nodded to Margaret when she stopped touching her face. Winona unbraided and braided her own and Margaret's hair. Mother disappeared for a while and when she returned, she looked almost like she always looked. Although she was redder in the face, than Margaret had ever seen her. *How does she look so neat and prim?* Margaret was too annoyed to wonder long.

They breakfasted on warmed over ham, potatoes, and pickles from the second jar. "Most likely, the strangest breakfast I have ever had!" Margaret's mother commented. "Also the tastiest." Ma nursed Isaac while she ate. Then she changed his dirty diaper. She had warmed up some water in the tin pail by setting it on their cooking rock. She sighed and wished aloud for some soap, as she washed it out in the luke-warm water.

"I think we should avoid Fort Ridgley. I listened to as much of the plans last night as I dared. Chief Taoyateduta plans on attacking the fort today. Which should mean that other places like the farms and towns could be safer. I think we should try to skirt the fort but make for New Ulm. What do you think?"

Both Margaret and her mother agreed. Margaret's mother asked, "Will we stay off the main routes again?"

"We should. Last night I saw a lot of prisoners. Women and children are being held as captives. We always do that. Then after the war, we exchange them for any prisoners our enemies hold. I didn't think they looked too happy to being held captive though. I'd like to avoid that fate for you if at all possible."

Margaret's mother nodded at these words. "Well, we'd best be on our way. Let's use these jars to carry some water with us in case we can't make it to a stream for mid-day meal."

Margaret filled the jars with water and tightened the lids. She placed them, wrapped in the burlap, into the pail. She added the left over ham, potatoes, and onions as well as the aprons, dish clothes, clean nappies, and Winona's bundle. The semi-clean nappy she spread on top. Hoping it would dry cleaner than it looked. She'd have liked to leave it, but they might need it. Margaret retrieved her damp petticoat and put it on. She helped Winona put out their fire, scatter the ashes and return the stone to the river. They brushed out their tracks. They knew that, if someone looked carefully, they would see signs of their camp. Winona hoped they wouldn't look too carefully.

Winona led the way to the rise. She took the lead and the bucket. Margaret took the rear just as they had yesterday. Whether they were to be killed or taken hostage, it would be best not to be caught.

Margaret adjusted her shawl, and continued to pull the grasses up behind their path. It was hard bending over so much. The grass was wet and didn't like to stay up. Her hands were raw and bleeding from yesterday's work. Winona called to her, told her not to worry. The rain had beaten down a lot of the grass. Even an experienced warrior would have trouble deciding which beaten down grasses were so because of passing feet and which had been flattened in the storm. Margaret was happy to drop this unpleasant task. As she only had to follow her mother now, she let her mind wander and think about all that Winona had told her.

New Ulm was their best hope. They could make it there by tonight if they were not forced to hide too much . . . or caught.

Her mother looked so much better than yesterday. Margaret was glad to see that, but she was very worried about her baby brother. She had never known him to be this quiet. She worried that he was ill or . . . well what else could he be but ill. He was not squawking, or grizzling like he usually did. He was just not himself. He did not seem cold or to be running a fever when she held him. He made eye contact with her, but he seemed very grave when he was awake. Margaret caught Winona's eyes once and wondered aloud if an infant could know of the danger they were in. Winona had shrugged, as if she thought it possible but did not have the energy to focus much on it at the moment.

Margaret quickly tired of walking, and her hands hurt from pulling the grass up yesterday. Looking at the cuts, she imagined they had left behind a bloody path. That would be quite the opposite of hiding their tracks. The rain of last night made the grass wet and slippery. Her skirts were sodden as were her mother's. Winona's leggings were wet but they seemed to bother her less than her own wet skirts.

Just as Margaret was getting well and truly frustrated, Winona interrupted her dark and gloomy thoughts. "There's a wagon track ahead. Do you think we should follow it? It would make the walking easier, and it is headed in the direction we want to go."

That brightened her thoughts. They wouldn't be walking through wet grass. "Yes. Let's follow it. We can duck into the prairie grass if we hear someone." Margaret said. They looked at Mother, and she nodded encouragingly. Margaret was exhausted already. She wanted nothing more than to lie down in a quiet place until all of this went away. How could she be this tired already? The sun was not even halfway to noon. Today was going to be a long day.

Chapter 11

They Meet a Wagon

WINONA FELT HERSELF TIRE WITH EACH STEP. Margaret and her mother seemed to have slowed down as well. She was wondering if they should find a good hiding place and rest for a while. Then she heard a wagon. She pushed Margaret and her mother into the grass and pulled it back up behind them. A wagon should be safe. Dakota rarely used them, but nothing was sure anymore. She forced them all to lie down, and then crouched up a little to peer through the grass. If it was a war party they would stay hidden. If, however, it was a wagon of settlers Margaret or her mother could find out some news. Perhaps they would have room in the wagon? Perhaps they could ride with them? They were all so tired. It would be nice to ride for a bit.

Margaret heard the wagon, too. She hoped the wagon carried German families. Maybe there would be room for her mother and Isaac. She watched Winona and when she nodded, Margaret knew she needed to stand and greet the settlers with the wagon. She stood slowly, worried that she would be shot at any moment. It scared her so badly that she thought her knees were going to collapse and no one would see her anyway.

Two men pulled the wagon, not horses or oxen. Men. A handful of women and children walked behind it. Margaret looked

70

behind her and gestured to Winona to stay hidden. Her mother stood and, holding Isaac to her with one hand, she held Margaret's hand with the other. The men stopped, the women stopped, and the children stopped. Everyone looked at Margaret and her mother. It was unbelievably quiet. Margaret broke the silence and asked how they were doing and what had happened to them.

One of the men who were pulling the wagon answered her. "We were attacked. You look worse for wear so you must be running from the Indians too. Was your husband killed, ma'am? The Dakota came and told us to get out. If we gave them our guns, they wouldn't kill us. We tried to hitch up our horses, but the Indians took them too. We were lucky. Some of our neighbors aren't with us anymore. We have a few things, and some injured in the wagon. We're headed to Fort Ridgley. The soldiers have guns, big guns. We'll be safe there. The soldiers will protect us." The farmer finished and the quiet echoed with his words.

"Is this the road to the fort then?" Margaret's mother asked.

"We sure hope so," the man replied. "We've been wanting to keep to the side trails rather than the roads. I reckon the Indians will be out in large force on the main roads. Why they attacking? Do you know? Well, we don't have time to stand in the open and talk about it. We best get to safety. You join in behind us. Two women out on the prairie by themselves ain't safe. You'll be better with our group."

"No we can't," Margaret's mother replied. "I have to return to my homestead. My husband may be injured. He'll be needing me."

Margaret gaped at her mother. The families did too. Margaret knew what these people didn't. Ma was choosing to stay with Winona. She felt safer with her. Margaret did too. Safer than they would be with the farmers and their wagon. Well, that was an interesting turn of events in Margaret's estimation.

"Don't do it, lady," One of the other men warned. "He's dead, sure as anything. Your husband. Hate to say it, but you'll be dead too if you go looking for 'im. The Dakota are killing women and children or worse." He looked at her for a long time. Although she nodded her understanding, she repeated her desire to find her husband.

The men reached for the tongue of the wagon and started to pull away. The small party walked by without a wave or a friendly parting. Margaret did not know who they were. They had not introduced themselves. But then neither had she and her mother. *War takes away all politeness*, Margaret thought.

As she waited with her mother for them to be out of sight, she asked Ma what could be worse than death?

"Many things," her mother replied and tightened her grip on baby Isaac. "Many things," she muttered again, more to herself this time.

After a while, long after the wagon and survivors had disappeared, Winona rose out of the prairie. Even though Margaret knew she would, it spooked her just the same how quietly Winona could move. Winona suggested they find a place to rest for a while and Margaret's mother agreed.

Winona worried that the wagon and its slow moving procession through the prairie would attract a roving band of warriors. She knew her own band had not learned of Taoyateduta's orders. They would not have listened anyway, Winona felt. Which meant they were still out here on the prairie ravaging homes and farms.

She led her small, quiet group down closer to the Minnesota River. They found a tree to rest under. Winona always felt safer under a tree. She could not explain why but she did. They ate and drank from one of the jars of water. Winona did not wish to go any closer to the river. The Dakota would cross it somewhere to get to Fort Ridgley, and she did not want to take any chances. She looked at Margaret and her mother. They were tired, sunburned, bug bitten, and exhausted. She had to admit that she did not feel any better herself. Even after eating the potatoes, ham, and onions they had brought in their tin pail. She simply felt empty.

Could they afford a few more minutes of rest? Margaret's mother made the decision for her. She changed Isaac's nappy and instructed Margaret to rinse it out and spread it somewhere to dry. Winona took it from her and carried it to the river, careful to stay hidden. She rinsed the disgusting cloth and brought it back, laying it over the tree branch close to the trunk of the tree. *Why white cloth?* wondered Winona. Green or brown would be so much better. Why not use a proper cradleboard with moss for the babe? These settlers were such a mystery.

Margaret's mother had stretched out next to Isaac, he lay on her shawl and was giggling and wiggling his arms and legs, completely oblivious to the peril they were in. She saw Margaret's relief that Isaac was all right and behaving like most babes should. Winona felt some relief herself, perhaps it would all be all right as well, perhaps it was all over and they would arrive at New Ulm in time to hear about peace negotiations. With that happy thought, Winona lay down close to Isaac and fell asleep immediately.

Margaret stared at Winona and felt like shouting, "She does sleep!" Winona had slept so little since yesterday morning. Was it only yesterday? Margaret had started to believe her friend might not be quite human. Margaret sat down with her back resting against the tree trunk. With Winona, and her mother both asleep, it was up to her to stand guard. But she chose to stand guard sitting down. Baby Isaac was still awake, kicking his legs gleefully and making the happy contented sounds she knew so well. Eventually, he tired of his toes and fell asleep.

Unfortunately Margaret drifted off too. She awoke to a strange feeling that she was being watched. Though she couldn't help the intake of breath, she held as still as she could, then cautiously opened her eyes. A few feet in front of her was a Dakota warrior. He wore no shirt, just leggings and had war paint on his chest and face. He had a leather band around his forehead with feathers standing behind his head. Her first instinct was to scream, but she bit her tongue and watched him instead. He was looking at Winona, who was already awake and sitting up. She gestured to all three of them and then her own chest repeatedly. She spoke to him, but Margaret did not know the words she was saying. She silently cursed herself for not understanding more Dakota.

Winona showed the brave her knife, the knife she had used last night to slice the potatoes. The brave smiled, even seemed to chuckle, then he said something and patted Winona on the head. He melted into the grass by their tree. He did not make a noise. One minute he was there and the next he was gone. Margaret didn't know what to do so she pressed her eyes shut.

Had she dreamt this? Was Winona plotting against them? Why? Had the warrior followed them? It was not her brother Brown Wing. Who could it be? Was there a bounty to bring in settlers? Margaret's eyes popped open at that thought. Bounties were paid for a lot for prisoners. She'd heard of this before in school. Winona wasn't looking at Margaret, so Margaret closed her eyes again and pretended to be sleeping. Margaret's stomach felt queer. Like it did yesterday, all unbalanced. What if Winona was not who she thought she was. What if the reason they were not going to Ridgley was to get Winona a higher bounty? Perhaps they should have gone with the others. Oh, this was confusing, how did she know what was right, when everything kept changing?

She decided she needed to be more vigilant and she needed to tell Mother this as soon as she could. They had trusted Winona for so long. Should they still trust her? Or had something changed?

"Wake up!" Winona hissed into Margaret's ear. "Watcher was just here. I think he believed my story, but I cannot be sure. We need to be gone from here soon. In case he went to get his friends and come back."

"What are you talking about?" Margaret asked, rubbing her arm where Winona gripped it. "Who is Watcher? Who are his friends?"

"Watcher was at your farm. He was with the braves who . . . Well, they were the ones who . . . I mean it was not him. It was the youngest with them who did it. I heard them bragging. But Watcher—that isn't his name, but I call him that—he was there. I was sure he saw me by the tree watching. I ran into him at Taoyateduta's village last night, and now he's here. He said our tracks were too easy to follow. He said he could not figure out why a Dakota girl was making such a mess."

"What did you tell him?" Margaret could not keep the bitterness out of her voice. For Winona to know this brave who snuck into their rest spot. This seemed too much of a coincidence.

"I told him you were my prisoners. That I found you on the prairie and was trying to find a shallow place to ford the river or to find a boat since white women cannot swim."

"He believed you?" Margaret thought this would be unlikely, if the brave had been tracking them and seen their attempts to pull up the grass behind them.

"He seemed to. He chided me for making such a trail. I thought we were doing such a good job. I don't know that he really believed me, though. It felt like how you believe someone who is telling you something you want to believe. Like when Father or Mother says everything is going to be all right. You want to believe it. Do you know what I mean?"

"Yes, I really do." Margaret answered. She really wanted to believe in Winona. She really did. But could she? Did friendship, her friendship with Winona, matter more to Winona than family and tribe. Margaret was not sure. The fact that the brave had left, well, that said something didn't it?

Margaret suddenly realized that Winona was looking at her. She was waiting for her to say something. Waiting for her to believe her? What choice did Margaret have? She would not last on the prairie without her. She needed to believe in Winona, but she would have to tell Mother as well. "We should go." Margaret answered Winona's question. "You're right. He could bring back more warriors. He may wish to capture us himself. Who would believe a weak Dakota girl like you could capture such a strong girl like me!" Margaret offered Winona a weak smile and her hand. Winona pulled her up and together they woke Margaret's mother.

Chapter 12

They Find the Wagon

Margaret sat very close to her mother at their next rest break. Winona went to see if she could find any food or signs of Dakota war parties. Margaret told her mother what had happened. Margaret wondered aloud if they should strike out on their own. "But I'm not sure. Winona could be our only hope. She couldn't be doing all this just to turn us in. But is blood thicker than friendship? Is it too much to expect of her? To turn her back on everything and every one?"

Her mother looked at her and said simply, "You're correct. Winona's our only hope. If she plans to trade us or sell us, she'll do so. I don't believe she's doing all this to trade us in later. I think you saw what she described. I know you're scared. I'm scared too. If we live through this, it's because of Winona. Your fear's feeding false reasoning. It's the same as what anger did to the young Dakota men. It blinds eyes to what's right. It turns ears against the truth. You only hear what you want to hear. It's all right to be scared, but Winona's been a friend for years. She came to find us. She left her family for you. She saved us. I doubt it was to take us prisoner."

Margaret felt deeply chastised and mumbled a response. Ma was right. Of course she always was. Margaret went to sit by herself for a bit. Winona came back, empty-handed. They ate the rest of the ham. All the potatoes and onions were gone. Winona carved all the meat off of the bone. It was cured. She said. They could eat it without cooking it. Margaret was too hungry to argue. They drank the water from the jars. They had refilled these at the river. Now both were empty. Empty and with a ham bone in their bucket, they got up to keep walking.

This cycle of walking and resting repeated itself until Margaret lost count. The walks felt longer and longer. The rests became shorter and less frequent. She knew that was this might just be an impression brought on by exhaustion, but she was starting to feel too numb to care about much.

The air turned hazy, Margaret could smell smoke. They walked by large burned sections of fields and farmsteads. Isaac fussed more today than he had yesterday. He did not cry, but he was unhappy and let everyone know in a whimpering, grating cry that was weak and pitiful. Margaret wondered if her mother was unable to nurse well after all the walking and the miserable night. Her mother said she was frightened. Would that emotion hurt her milk? Was Isaac feeling frightened because Mother was?

Margaret wished for it to all be over. She just wanted to lie down for a very long time in a bed, but the ground kept looking better and better. They were following a set of wagon tracks. She wasn't sure if it was the same set as earlier. It was a well-used trail, and they walked in the grassy section in the middle so as to leave fewer footprints. Winona was still mad that Watcher had said she was leaving tracks like a white man.

The sun was overhead so that Margaret could no longer tell if they were still going northeast or not. The sun beat down on her sunburned face and hands, she tried to wrap her hands in her apron but the insides hurt where the grass had cut yesterday. All in all, Margaret was miserable. She knew she should feel more grateful at being alive, but somehow she couldn't muster the energy for gratitude. She was too hurt. Too tired. Too hungry. Too thirsty.

Suddenly Winona stopped and gestured wildly for them to hide in the grass by the tracks.

Margaret could not hear anything but she gratefully sank down in the long grass. Mother lay down next to her. She handed her Isaac. Margaret placed him in her lap. The baby seemed as tired as she felt. Winona whispered that she could see a wagon ahead. She said she would approach it but felt they should stay here. Margaret agreed by nodding, and Winona was gone.

Winona approached the still wagon carefully. The settlers may have abandoned it and their wounded. Or they may be near by resting. She waited but could hear no sounds besides the droning of the flies. She edged closer. When she saw the bodies she stopped. Then she turned back. They were dead. All of them. She could do nothing for them. They had been alive this morning. She had heard some of them speak. Now they would never speak again.

Winona said nothing but led Margaret and her mother through the prairie till they were past the wagon of death. Then she told them what she had found, that everyone in the wagon party was dead. She started to weep. She said it was her brother who had caused all of this.

"Will this never end? What could unarmed settlers do to brave warriors? Why is this happening? Why are my people doing this?" Winona continued to sob. Margaret could scarcely understand her words. "We will never get to safety. Where is it safe? The soldiers are being attacked. The unarmed are being attacked. This is not the Dakota way? Why is this happening? We will die on this prairie. We will walk in circles for years. Our bodies will die of starvation. Our bones will shrivel from the heat and turn to dust!" Winona stomped in a circle, kicking small stones, sticks, and the occasional tufts of grass.

Margaret was fearful to reach out to her. Winona looked mad enough to kick her too. She stood with her hands clasping and unclasping. It hurt her cut hands to do this. But Margaret welcomed the pain. She hoped it would clear her thoughts and help her find the right words to say to Winona.

Margaret's mother spoke before Margaret could figure out what to say. "Winona, this is not going to go on forever. You said it yourself. We simply need to stay alive and stay moving. We have a better chance to be alive if we're moving. Now, we need you—which is the way to New Ulm?"

Both Winona and Margaret looked at her mother with open mouths. Mother was not known for thinking strong thoughts, let alone voicing them. *Something's happening here*, Margaret thought. *It's like we've all become different from who we once were.*

"We can't control what others are doing, and this is a terrible place to be right now, but we're still safe and alive because of you, Winona. We can't change everything, but we can keep going. We can save ourselves. We're all we have. But right now that'll be enough."

After saying that, Mother turned and started walking in the direction they had been going. Winona wiped her eyes with the end of her braids. She reached for Margaret's hand and they continued along the wagon tracks. Winona whispered in Margaret's ear loudly enough for her Mother to hear. "I did not know she had that in her!" From the back it looked as if Mother's spine stiffened a bit, her head lifted and her pace quickened. Whether this was from pleasure or anger, Margaret didn't know.

Although Winona felt a little better, it wasn't much. Her mind whirred again. It was as if a whirly wind were stuck in her brain. Why were the Dakota warriors still attacking innocent farmers, women and children when Taoyateduta had told them not to? He had told them where to attack. Why were they not attacking the soldiers at Fort Ridgley? What if Fort Ridgley had already fallen?

80

There were thousands of Dakota warriors. If they had all worked together, the fort might no longer stand. What might that mean for New Ulm? Could the Dakota be winning? Had they won the fort? Was this why they were attacking the farms? The soldiers would come out of Fort Snelling, Taoyateduta had said, they would pour out of it with their horses and guns. What if Long Knives—Henry Sibley—would be their general?

Winona mentally shuddered. Perhaps it was just her band, not following orders and marauding on the prairie. Her father disliked working with anybody, even Taoyateduta. They were getting close to the fort. If Winona altered their original course, they could come up closer and see what was happening.

"Margaret, should we continue to New Ulm? Or should we try the fort? It still might be safer. If the bands are still out here attacking and killing women and children, they might not be attacking the fort or the fort may have fallen. But the fort has cannons. I cannot decide, what makes the most sense?"

Margaret mumbled an, "I don't know." As they got closer to the fort, she felt their answer would be made for them. She voiced her thought that the attack would be noisy, that they should hear it. Just as she said that, they became aware of a low rumble like thunder but on a cloudless afternoon. Winona and Margaret saw the smoke together. Margaret pointed, "That's Fort Ridgley, isn't it?"

Winona and her mother both nodded. They looked unbelievably disappointed.

"All right then," said Margaret. "We go to New Ulm."

Chapter 13

Another Farm, Another Family

WINONA WHISPERED TO MARGARET that they should use a cornfield as cover and go as far away as possible from the fort before swinging around it to reach New Ulm. Margaret gave her a confused look, "Why go so far back. The Dakota should all be attacking the fort. This area should be deserted of warriors."

"No," Winona replied. "The Dakota fight in small independent groups. They do not fight in long rows as your soldiers do. Some of the Dakota will join the battle at Ridgley after they have plundered and killed the farmers and their families. They will be lighting fires to farm buildings and crops. They will light fire to hay stacks to draw out the soldiers from the fort as well. Remember, the Dakota wish to drive all of the whites from Dakota lands forever. Taoyateduta knows the fort is the starting point. He says it is the gate to the East. However, many are not agreeing with him. We need to stay hidden to stay alive."

"Why don't the Dakota fight all together? We read in the newspapers how the battles are fought in the South. Remember what I read to you, how the men are all lined up and then walk in to the other armies together?" Margaret wondered aloud.

"That is your way of fighting. Our way is more independent. Men advance and fall back. Each trusts his own fighting spirit. It will be hard for the soldiers to fend off a strong Dakota attack. As each fights on his own, the soldiers and the fort will be attacked from all sides."

"They will win the fort then. It doesn't even have walls. Pa told me that after his trip there."

"That is why I do not want us to get close." Winona continued, we will have a better chance if we go far from it and circle around."

Both girls fell quiet as they walked through the cornrows. It would be such a good crop this year. All this food on the prairie. Yet, the corn was unripe. The warehouse doors locked. So much could have been averted if only the doors would have been opened and the food distributed as promised.

Winona whispered, "We have to keep our promises." Margaret nodded. It was uncanny how alike she and Winona were. Winona seemed to read her mind.

"So much waste, Winona. All the hay so neatly stacked for winter. Now burned to the ground. Barns burned. Gardens and homes destroyed. If the Dakota do win, what will be left to be eaten in the winter? There's so little left?"

"They are not thinking of their bellies anymore. It is their pride that hurts more. If the Dakota win, will the whites allow Minnesota to return to them? Will your mother give up her land for my family?" Winona squeezed Margaret's hand while she spoke.

"Mother might. Father never would."

"Exactly. The men will not forgive this. Their pride will be hurt. The women will be unforgiving as well. Think of losing your husband, your son. How could you forgive that?"

"Forgiveness is for the living. Let's stay alive." Margaret let go of Winona's hand so they could walk more quickly single file through the cornrows.

Margaret sighed and continued to push through the corn, carefully and quietly. It would not do anyone any good if they left broken stalks of corn announcing their presence.

Winona stopped at the edge of the field. Like so many other farms, the one in front of her was smoldering. The fire must have been set this morning. There would be no food left, as the buildings were all smoking ruins.

Looking behind her, she saw Margaret's mother fall down again, exhausted, too exhausted to keep the pace Winona was setting. Pushing back into the cornfield, they all sat down for a while.

What could they do for food? Eating the green corn that grew all around them would give them stomach cramps. The ham was all gone except for the bone, which they carried, thinking it could make a watery ham soup later. They needed water. They were tired and out of food. They could not remain in the cornfield forever. Could they? Fingering the handle of her knife, she wondered what they should do.

Margaret suggested they search the ruined farm together. "The well must still be there. We might find a root cellar. The garden might have beans or peas that we can gather."

Telling Margaret's mother they were off to look for food and water, Winona took the jars out of the pail, still wrapped in burlap to keep them from clinking. Winona folded them into Margaret's apron. This left both Margaret and Winona's hands free. They walked doubled over to the smoking farmstead. Winona felt very exposed and vulnerable. Glancing over at Margaret, she could tell she felt the same.

Near the remains of the house, Margaret found a tin pail. Searching quickly she also found the stones of the well. The upper wooden contraption that lowered or raised the buckets of water was missing, burned out. Of course, the rope was burned as well.

Tossing a rock into the hole, Winona heard it splash very quickly. Removing the glass jars from her apron, Margaret set them aside. Then she removed her shoes and stockings. Using Margaret's stockings, as well as Winona's sash, they made an improvised well rope. Lowering the bucket in and carefully pulling it back up.

The first pail was slimy with ash. They dumped it and pulled another up another and another. Still pretty disgusting. On their fifth bucket, the water looked drinkable. After they drank their fill, they pulled up a sixth for Margaret's mother. Winona carried this back after warning Margaret to not get into any trouble. She was to stay quiet until Winona could get back to her.

Margaret made her way barefoot along the back of the ruined house. She could not find any sort of a trap door along the back or sides of it. Biting her lip to think, she looked around the farmstead. Seeing a small rise a hundred steps away she carefully walked over to it. Could they have dug into the side of the little hill to create their root cellar?

She walked over and crouched down to look around. Finally she saw what she was looking for: a small door. Pulling it out, she peered in. It was tiny, but it was most definitely a cellar. It was cool inside, the earth comforting on her bare toes.

There was a small beer keg and a linked rope of sausages. She could not possibly carry the keg, nor did she like the taste of beer. Looping the sausages over her shoulder she found some new potatoes and onions in a bin on the floor as well as a few carrots. Filling her apron with as much as it would hold, Margaret retreated quickly to their hiding spot.

Taking the most direct route, she went a different way than they had come earlier. She wished immediately that she hadn't when she saw the bodies. The entire family had been killed and their bodies pulverized so that only their clothes showed the men from the women. Margaret suddenly vomited all of the water she had so recently gulped down. Forgetting to be quiet, she ran sobbing to her mother.

Winona was too upset by her friend's cries to be excited at the food she had found. Margaret would not stop crying. Although her mother held her and said comforting words to her, she did not ask what was wrong. Her mother knew. Winona knew as well. Neither needed to be told.

Winona led them further into the cornfield. Finally Margaret was able to stop crying and settle down some. But she would not eat or drink. Winona worried about this. They needed to keep going and get past the fort or they would not make it to safety today, but she could tell that neither Margaret nor her mother were able to go on. Margaret cried herself to sleep. Her mother had baby Isaac unbundled and he was happily playing with his toes.

Winona bent the corn some to create a bit of a sunshade and lay down herself. They had left a lot of tracks. She hoped that the braves who had done all the earlier damage would not return and the ruined buildings would not attract any new attacks or searches.

Chapter 14

Camp Peaceful

MARGARET WOKE TO A LIGHT DRIZZLE. She looked at her mother and Winona. Both were watching her, concern in their eyes. Winona had returned to the farmstead and found Margaret's stockings and shoes. Winona's sash was around her waist again. Margaret pulled on her stockings and laced her shoes. She reached for the tin pail of water and drained half of it. Her mother gave her a piece of cold sausage. As Margaret chewed it, her mother drank more from the pail, offering the last to Winona before dumping the rest. Mother packed it with the sausage and some of the carrots, onions, and potatoes that had fallen out of her tied apron. Mother stood and with Margaret's help fastened a content Isaac into his shawl carrier. Margaret picked up the bucket of sausage and potatoes and followed Winona.

Quickly, they walked past the ruined farm. Using the wagon path, so as to not make new tracks, Winona led them past many more burned-out farms and smoldering haystacks. Some crops had been burned standing in the fields. This left them with little for a hiding place if someone came along their wagon trail.

The drizzle turned to rain, and Margaret felt even more miserable. *How can it be?* She wondered. *Each time, I find something new to make me feel even more exhausted, wet, tired, crabby, ornery, rotten, frustrated.* She continued to mumble to herself as she followed Winona.

Eventually, Winona left the wagon track and followed a small trail down to a creek. Sitting down, she removed her moccasins. Margaret helped her mother sit down and untied her boots for her. Removing her stockings, she then did her own and followed mother and Winona into the creek.

Winona walked along the middle of it for a while before crossing to the other side and led them under a tree with a lot of low drooping boughs to hide under. A willow, Margaret thought. Good shelter.

They were soaked. Winona brought out her fire starter kit and looked at Margaret. Her eyes questioned whether they could risk a small fire. Margaret's visible misery convinced her to gather some dry twigs to start a small blaze. Margaret went under other tree branches and gathered all the dry branches she could.

"The rain should keep the war parties at their own fires," Winona said almost as if she were speaking her thoughts aloud. "I'll sharpen some sticks for the sausages. See if you can find a flat stone by the creek. Keep you shoes off. You will make less tracks."

Fetching the pail after dropping off her large flat rock, she fetched water for her Mother and Winona to drink. She fetched another bucket for her mother to wash Isaac's face. Then a last bucket to warm by the fire. She took the dirty nappies down to the creek and rinsed them out. She hung them on a branch near the fire to dry.

It felt almost normal to fetch water, fetch wood and clean nappies. She watched Winona cut some willow branches from other bushes and use them to create an even more hidden spot. Then she went to the creek to erase any tracks to their hiding spot.

Margaret's mother pierced the potatoes using Winona's knife. She placed them in the new coals around the fire to cook. She told Margaret and Winona that she planned to cook half of them. They could eat cold cooked potatoes in the morning, but not cold raw potatoes. She smiled, the first one Margaret had seen since they had left her mother's kitchen days ago. It felt like months ago.

Margaret fetched a few more dry branches so they would have a good pile to last as long as the rain lasted. It felt good to be doing such regular chores and smell potatoes cooking. She almost felt like herself again. She could almost forget why they were here.

Winona never remembered eating so well. The rain kept up all the next day. Keeping the fire going helped fight off the mosquitoes. They spent the entire next day and night resting by their small fire in their tree encampment. The sausages cooked over the fire on small willow twigs. Their sizzling was the best sound Winona had heard in some time. The potatoes were creamy in the middle and crispy on the outside. There were so many she could throw away the charred outsides without feeling sad. The onions cooking on the rock in the middle made everything smell delicious. They ate to their heart's content, slept, gathered wood and water, ate and slept again.

Winona enjoyed doing the chores of camp with Margaret. It felt normal, calm. She had not realized how much terror she had been carrying inside her until it started raining and a calm settled in her brain. The rain washed over the prairie, erasing their tracks, quenching the fires raging where there used to be homes. It made her forget all of their troubles and their struggles. She felt like she could smile again.

Perhaps the rain would just keep coming. It had been so dry last year and gotten dry again this year.

"What if it could keep raining, long enough to dampen the warriors anger?" Margaret broke into her thoughts. "I'm wondering if God sent this rain to help end the war?"

"Or Wakantanka!" Winona answered testily, "Why must you always think your god is more powerful than mine?" Seeing the look on Margaret's face made Winona wish she could bring her sharp words back into her mouth. She'd spoken without thinking and was regretful immediately. The calm feeling they had all shared for the last day was gone. Winona mentally kicked herself. *Why can I never learn that the only one who listens to me is Margaret? Perhaps her mother too? Why can I not remember how easily words can hurt?*

"You're right, of course. You're always right, Winona. It has to be the Great Spirit. Our God is awfully busy right now down South!" With that retort, Margaret burst into one of her good-natured grins and went to collect more wood. They had run out of the dry pieces under the trees, and now had to lay out pieces by the fire to dry them in advance before they could burn them. Tending the fire was a lot of work but it kept the damp down. Truly, the fire made all of them feel better. As if there was not death and destruction outside of the trees.

As they worked, Margaret went back to her wondering aloud. "Do you think it could rain long enough for everyone to settle down? I mean the farmers, the Dakota, maybe they might start talking again instead of shooting first!"

"How can they?" Winona answered. "It is just us with our wishful thinking hoping that they will all come to their senses like an angry child after a tantrum. But can this go away this easily? Your mother, once she is recovered, will she not be mad at the braves who killed her son and most likely her husband?"

Margaret gasped, "I never wanted to think it, let alone say it, but you saw Jakob. He's dead. We both know my Pa. He'd run right in to shoot before thinking. He really is dead isn't he?"

"He most certainly is," Winona said sadly. "What will you do, once we are safe? Will you not be mad at the braves, at the men who did that? Maybe you will want them punished for what they did?"

"I don't think it's that easy. I don't think anyone deserved to die, but what does punishment do? Can you punish a brave and get my pa back? Of course not. Besides, Pa was mean. I may not want to hear that from anyone else, but he was hard on everyone, his own family too. I'm muddled now. I don't know what to think or what to say even. But you're right. No one will let this go away. Why are men so willing to kill others? Is it only men? Are there women warriors do you think?" Margaret questioned her friend.

"No, Dakota women are too smart to fight and white women don't know which end of a gun is the business end!" chortled Winona as she threw a stick at Margaret's foot, knowing she would dance away from it.

Margaret danced away easily but hurled her own stick, catching Winona off guard. Trying to dance away from it, Winona slipped in the wet grass and landed on her butt and started to laugh. Margaret bent over her to help pull her up and instead Winona pulled her down too. Both girls laughed until they cried.

But as they gathered the sticks and branches that had fallen tipsy turvy all over, Winona knew that the rain lasting forever, or everyone talking was simply wishful thinking. The braves' anger, the agents' anger and now the settlers' anger—all were like a pot taken off the fire. It may not look like it was boiling but it would burn anyone who tried to touch it.

The sun would shine again, and bloodshed would begin again until all the soldiers rode from Fort Snelling to squash the warriors. Winona knew that this much hurt would not be allowed to go away. The settlers would demand justice. No matter how mean Margaret's pa was, he did not deserve to die, and none of the rest of the settlers did either. Rage was being taken out on the wrong people. *Ahh, just like when I snapped at Margaret. I'm not mad at her, but the person I am mad at, isn't around. My anger flows in the wrong direction to the wrong person.*

Margaret woke to no rain. Dread settled into her stomach like a bad piece of meat. It turned and twisted her guts until she could taste bile. Worried she might vomit, she struggled to her feet and down to the creek. Washing her face, she tried to wash away her thoughts. The end of the rain meant the Dakota braves would resume their attacks on the fort and the countryside.

She drank some water, but it didn't settle her stomach, only gave it more juice to turn into bile. She pulled herself up from the creek and returned slowly to their campsite. They had not been here that long. Only a day and a half, but it had started to feel like home. She would think of it as Camp Peaceful. She thought of helping herself to one of their last potatoes. It was still a little warm from the ashes of the fire. It might settle her stomach, but it might not. Instead, she undid Winona's hair and using her fingers combed it and braided it again into the two plaits Winona liked to wear. Undoing Winona's bundle that she had carried with her for the last few days, Margaret pulled out the hair ribbons. She had given these to Winona a long time ago. They had been kept safely wrapped under the tree and now carried with them. It was time, Margaret felt, for Winona to wear them.

Winona fingered the ribbons. Then smiled at Margaret. "I'll make you a new sash. I always told you burying your treasures was safer than putting them under the bed. Why is it I'm always right?"

"At least you don't let it go to your head!" Margaret retorted. She was sad to think of her small box of treasures gone to ashes, but as Winona said, she would make her a new sash. Things could be replaced. Friends could not. She smiled at Winona and offered her a cold potato.

Winona turned up her nose at the potato. She braided Margaret's hair into the long single plait Margaret preferred. They both encouraged Margaret's mother to take her time, but to eat as much as she could.

Margaret changed Isaac's nappy and bundled him back into his shawl arrangement. When her mother was ready, Margaret tied the shawl around mother's back. Isaac was burbling happily, Mother looked like herself again. *A day of lying around sure worked wonders on the body and spirit,* Margaret thought. Hopefully their strength would hold until they got someplace outside of the fighting.

Margaret wrapped the last of the potatoes and sausage in the dishtowel, and then she laid the bundle of clean nappies into the tin pail. The dishtowel of food went on top. They left the other pail by the ashes of the fire. They really did not need two.

Swinging it by her side, she started to follow her mother, who was following Winona. As they left, Winona did not even try to disguise their camp. She did ask Margaret to pull up the grass, and wipe the prints away from the muddy parts so their tracks from the creek would not give away their direction.

Margaret felt like she could walk all day today. She was rested and fed. Although the fear came over her as soon as they left their hideout, she calmed it with the thought that they had made it this long and this far. It was an achievement. She looked at Winona and they shared a small grin.

Margaret's ears burned with shame thinking of how foolish she had been not to trust Winona earlier. Was it just two mornings ago? It felt as if it were weeks ago. How had such awful thoughts entered her mind? Winona was her savior. Mother, Isaac, and Winona were all she had left. Her older brother was dead. Her father likely was dead as well. "It's just us," she whispered to herself.

Chapter 15

To New Ulm

WINONA CONTINUED IN HER NORTHEASTERLY CIRCLE. She was sure this would lead them to New Ulm. The rain had so beaten down the grass that they could step right on it, without leaving the broken trail they had the last two days they had traveled. When Winona felt they had walked far enough north to get around the fort, she turned them due east.

No smoke on the horizon. She could not hear any guns. She stopped and laid her ear to the ground, but she could hear nothing. They would come closer to the river as they walked straight east. This might bring them closer to warriors on their way to Fort Ridgley but she was hoping to get to New Ulm as quickly as possible.

They rested for a bit and devoured the rest of the cold but cooked sausage and potatoes. Their tin bucket was a good deal lighter now. They had left the jars at the farm of death. Winona thought they made too much noise anyway. They would just have to reach water before their next rest.

After resting, Winona found a well-used wagon track. She followed it. She was sure this was the main route from the fort to New Ulm. She hoped the exposure to gain speed would be worth it. Along the way they passed many burned fields, farms, and haystacks reduced to ashes. Winona was struck again by the thought that the Dakota were going to starve no matter what the outcome of the war.

Winona was startled by a loud noise and forced them to hide in the cornfield that bordered the road. Thankfully, it had not been burned as so many they had passed. She stayed hidden trying to determine what the noise was. It was low and intermittent.

Finally, Margaret suggested, "Cannon fire?" They both looked in the direction of Fort Ridgley. The attack had started. The cannon fire carried to them but it was muffled compared to the other day. "We were closer before." Margaret answered the unsaid question in Winona's mind.

They could see tremendous plumes of smoke darkening the sky. Margaret reached out and squeezed Winona's hand. Whether to reassure, to hurry them on, or because she was scared, Winona was not sure. Feeling vulnerable and scared they hurried on their way.

More farms were located here than where Margaret's family homesteaded. The number that had been burned seemed to be declining, as they kept heading east. This cheered Winona. The braves may not have gotten this far. This also allowed them standing fields of corn for cover.

Winona was particularly pleased to see all the haystacks standing unburned. She felt a playful urge to climb them and slide down. She and Margaret had often gotten yelled at for doing just that as children. Still it looked odd to have so much intact right next to the devastation they had been walking through. But the homes here seemed to be deserted. Winona had no desire to explore. Neither did the others. Their one thought was New Ulm and safety.

Reaching the river, Winona ground her teeth as she tried to think. Not only could white ladies not run, she doubted that Margaret's mother could swim. The current was not too swift, but the rains had swollen the river and would make it more difficult to cross.

"Look!" Margaret pointed. "There's a boat. We could use that, couldn't we?"

Winona agreed, what a great piece of luck. It was a tad leaky but it would work. Margaret clambered in and took Isaac from her mother. Then her mother climbed in and Winona handed her their pail, then took off her clothes and handed them in. Without her telling them, Winona was pleased to note that Margaret and her mother sat in the wet bottom of the boat and stayed as low as they could. Winona pushed the boat out into the current and using all her strength got it to the other side. She let the current take them down river some, hoping that if anyone was watching it would look like an empty boat adrift.

Reaching the other side, she pushed and then pulled it onto the bank, hurriedly getting dressed under the trees. Winona realized she was shaking, whether from exertion or fear, she didn't know.

On this side, there was also less destruction. They passed the farmhouses as quickly as they could, except one. Margaret's mother handed Isaac to Margaret and ran to the clothesline. Clothes still hung as if waiting for the end of the day to be brought in. She grabbed a dress and petticoat from the line and told Winona to put them on. "I'm worried a settler might shoot you before listening to what you've done. They're damp from the rain, but put them over your clothes."

Winona refused at first. "No, no. I am just going to get you close to New Ulm. I am not going to go into the town. I will see you there safely and then return to my family."

"I know that's your plan. But just in case, it'd be better not to be shot. The settlers who have escaped this are bound to be jumpy. If you're in a petticoat and dress, from a distance we will appear as three white women, seeking shelter." Margaret's mother answered. She reached out her hands for Isaac. Margaret helped her fasten the shawl again. "Margaret, help Winona fasten the buttons."

Winona agreed to put on the dress, but she handed the petticoat to Margaret with a grin. Margaret, who smiled at the memory of the petticoat and the mosquitoes, handed it back, saying the dress didn't look right without a petticoat under it.

"I can see your split skirt and leggings through it. Put both on. Hand me your knife." As Winona watched, Margaret split the seam a few inches in both the skirt of the dress and the petticoat underneath. Although it was now three layers deep, Winona could still reach in to retrieve her knife without too much work.

"Thank you." Winona whispered to Margaret.

The noise of wagons suddenly interrupted the quiet. All three of them dropped to the ground. Winona clumsily reached through her layers of clothing and rested her hand on her knife. It seemed as if there were hundreds of men approaching, with wagons, pulled by horses. They were making such noise, it hurt Winona's ears after their enforced quiet of the last days.

They stayed hidden until they heard the men hallooing for anyone who was hurt.

"We're from New Ulm! Wir sind nach Neu Ulm! Anyone there? Jeiderman heir? We have a doctor! Wir haben einen Doktor!"

The men repeated this call as they walked closer and closer to the cornrows, where the friends were hiding. Men ran ahead and looked into the houses and barns as they approached. Finally, Margaret jumped up and waved her arms. Her mother stood as well. Winona slowly got to her feet and followed hesitantly. They walked up to the men and were besieged with questions:

"Are there anymore with you? Who are you? Are you wounded? Are you all right? Do you have news about the fort? Do you know what has been happening on the agency?"

Margaret replied negatively to most of their questions. "It's just us," she replied. A doctor, Doctor Mayo, came over and looked them over. Not seeing anything serious, they were helped into one of the wagons. However, instead of turning back towards New Ulm and safety, the wagons went in the opposite direction, over the prairie they had just walked. Seeing their distress, a man stated, "We want to see if there are any more survivors. Then we will turn back to New Ulm. We thought we would find more, but all we have found is you."

Winona was getting a couple of odd looks but not as many as she had feared. A few of the men were half-breeds. One man came over to tell Winona she was lucky. The war parties had been killing the half-breeds at the agency just like the whites. His name was Joseph. He had decided to help New Ulm and keep people safe. Just as it looked like Winona had done.

Winona asked if he had been in battle. She spoke in Dakota, but he answered in English, "I fought the day before yesterday. The rain kept the war parties away. We were defending the town against the attacks.

"I don't understand why they are attacking the town, or the settler's homes. The traditional Dakota are starving, but they have not been taking food, just killing. Why kill those who have not harmed you? Some who had helped and fed Dakota are dead by their hands. Why?" Joseph looked into Winona's eyes as if he hoped the answer was there.

She shook her head, not trusting herself to speak. Her band, her brother and father were killing those who had once opened a door and fed a hungry Dakota man. She could not understand it either, how could she expect anyone else to?

Joseph went off to continue to search with the men. She noticed that they were not calling in Dakota. They would not be looking for Dakota survivors. Not that there would be any. The braves always pulled their wounded or dead warriors back with them as they left the battle. To leave the dead was to show the enemy that they had hurt you.

Chapter 16

No Other Survivors

MARGARET FELT SUCH RELIEF TO BE IN THE WAGON. Pulled by horses no less. But it felt very wrong to be traveling away from New Ulm instead of towards it. Still, if there was anyone else out there like themselves, she wanted them to have safety too. The men had water and crackers, which they shared as they continued to search.

The men continued to yell as they walked. Margaret thought she should tell them they were already making enough racket for folks to find them. Friend or foe. The wagons, the horses, and all the sounds all the men walking made tremendous noise. They didn't need to shout. But she thought it best not to interrupt.

Perhaps it made them feel better. Like how Margaret yelled at Mabel, the cow after it swatted her with her tail. Or how she yelled at a chicken after it pecked her arm. You couldn't stop what had happened but shouting made you feel in control again. After a while, she leaned into her mother and fell asleep.

When she woke, the prairie was completely silent. The wagons were all stopped. The men were standing still, not speaking. What was it? Margaret wondered, what's happened? Then she realized that the cannon fire that had accompanied them all day was gone. She looked around wondering if the quiet was a good or a bad thing. What did it mean if the cannons had stopped firing? Everyone else seemed to be wondering the same question. The wagons, as if the drivers had all had the same thought, turned in a wide circle off the road and headed back the way they had come.

"We're turning around, heading back to New Ulm, lest the Dakota attack again while most of the armed men are on the prairie." Joseph came by and told people in their wagon.

"Again?" Margaret shouted with alarm. "New Ulm has already been attacked!" She startled many of the men into looking at her.

Winona nodded, as did Joseph. Now Margaret realized that Joseph had been defending New Ulm. Winona, Margaret, and her mother had been counting on New Ulm being safe. Was there any safe place? Where could they go to be safe if everywhere was being attacked and all at once?

Winona had said the Dakota warriors, if they worked together could defeat the fort. She had not thought they would attack together as all the burned homes suggested the raiding parties were not fighting with Taoyateduta. Margaret wondered if the quiet from the fort meant the Dakota had won. Would they attack New Ulm again? Would they use the cannon against the town?

So many men had gone to the War in the South, and so many more had been killed. Here with the wagons, there were a hundred or so armed men. They said, they were almost all New Ulm had. Could a hundred hold off the Dakota if they attacked?

Perhaps having Winona put on a dress had been a mistake. Maybe she and mother should have changed their clothes. Could they keep hiding if they got off the wagons now? She looked at Winona and could tell she was thinking some of the same thoughts.

Winona's eyes were dancing, as if all she wanted to do was leap from the wagon and run. Her hand was holding her knife through the layers of skirts. She looked as if she would bolt at any moment.

But then Margaret saw her look at Isaac. He was lying down next to where they were sitting. His arms and legs were kicking and he was blowing bubbles with his mouth. Margaret watched as Winona's mouth hardened, her eyes stopped their darting. She took her hand away from her knife and started rubbing her jaw with her hand.

"No, for better or worse, we are headed to New Ulm. We are together. Isaac and your mother cannot keep hiding. The men might not let us leave." As Winona finished her sentence, Margaret made eye contact with Joseph. He nodded almost imperceptibly. They had to stay.

Winona noticed the signs of the Dakota attack as soon as they drew to the outskirts of town. Buildings were burned, windows broken out of stone buildings. She had never been to the town of New Ulm, like Margaret, but so many destroyed buildings meant the Dakota had gotten very close in their attacks.

All the buildings on the outskirts of town were burned, but as they neared the center she saw the barricades. The townspeople had put up fences and piles of wood. This was the line they had held. That had kept the Dakota from taking over the town.

She wondered which bands had attacked New Ulm. Was Taoyateduta leading at Fort Ridgley? Shakopee leading the braves in their attacks here? Were both attacks part of Taoyateduta's plan? Had her father stopped his marauding on the helpless farmsteaders and assumed a leadership role in the attack at Ridgley? Winona shrugged at her thoughts.

She said to Margaret, "I cannot imagine Taoyateduta authorizing an attack on New Ulm. He has stated over and over that the soldiers and the government were whom the Dakota had to defeat. Settlers, women, and children would not help the struggle. If the Dakota mounted the attack we see here, they are not following Taoyateduta's orders. And if Taoyateduta is not being listened to, if the tribes and bands are not working together, the Dakota are lost.

"Their only chance for a victory, whatever it might look like, was to allow a great leader to lead. If the braves decided not to follow, there was nothing a leader could do."

"But don't the braves understand that they have to trust their leaders? When the army gives a command, soldiers follow it. Why are they not following Little Crow? They wanted his approval so much at the beginning." Margaret had interrupted Winona without thinking. Then got quiet so Winona would continue. They were speaking softly in the back of the wagon as it drew closer to the stables.

"Power is given in the Dakota way. It is not like in the white army where you have to follow orders whether you wished to or not. Father and brother can decide not to fight. They can choose to fight elsewhere. I do not know which way is right. But I think the Dakota will lose. So perhaps the white way is the better way to win"

Margaret, her mother, and Winona were helped down from the wagon by the stables. They were directed to a stone house for some soup and bread. The house was in the center of town, and it had a deep cellar with stone walls. Many of the women and children of the town were gathered inside the house, or close by so they could hide in the basement of stone. Margaret's mother handed Isaac to Winona and went to help with the cooking and feeding the town's inhabitants and refugees.

Along the side of the house, great pots rested over cook fires. Long tables had been set up where the men, women and children could eat. The town was trying to get through an evening meal when they arrived. Winona and Margaret were hungry. But they felt it would cause too many stares to go through the line. Instead they huddled next to a wall and watched the townspeople.

Winona was scared that she had made a terrible mistake. Many women looked at her with such hatred, as if they would like to murder her. While she held Isaac she felt safe, thinking they would not hurt the baby. *Is this why Margaret's mother gave him to me? To keep me safe?*

Margaret rebraided Winona's hair. Borrowing a couple of hairpins from another girl, she pinned Winona's hair up. Hopefully, this would make her look older and perhaps, she tried to convince herself, whiter? She did not think it would work. Both girls were getting hostile glances from the women. None from the men. They consumed their food without so much as a mumbled thank you and then disappeared from their view.

The girls rested against the side of the house for a while. Margaret noticed the quiet. There was some conversation, but it was in hushed tones. It seemed as if there were hundreds if not a thousand people gathered around a handful of stone buildings. This many people gathered to eat together should be loud with conversation. The beer barrels were out. Ordinarily this would mean a party, loud singing, and perhaps some dancing. But not today, the men consumed large mugs with their meal, but not one man was singing or smiling. Not one child was laughing. All waited with hushed tones for whatever would come. Mother came by with two tin plates full of potato stew.

"There might even be some meat in it," she said as she handed them to Margaret. "Eat up. I ate before I started helping." She took Isaac out of Winona's arms so Winona could eat as well.

Margaret wondered if her mother really had eaten first, but she was too hungry to fret about it. There was a piece of bread for each girl, and Margaret used hers to sop up every drop of the stew.

"Feel better?" her mother asked. Margaret had to admit she did. Margaret offered to carry the plates back to where the cook pots were now turning into soapy water to wash things up. She felt that it would be a bad idea to let Winona out of her sight, but she knew her Mother would keep her safe. After pitching in to help wash the tin plates and wooden spoons, she asked if she could have a clean mug for water. A woman, who was wiping the tables down, gestured with her chin to the tin and pewter tankards the men had used earlier.

"They're all clean. There's a pump for water around back." Margaret thanked her and grabbing two, filled them with clean water from the pump. The water tasted delicious as she drank two mugs full. Then she brought the two brimming with water back to Winona and her mother. They drank, asked for more, which Margaret was happy to fetch. Margaret then washed the mugs, said thank you again to the helpful lady, who nodded her chin at her again.

Then Margaret rejoined Winona and her mother, and voiced her thought of finding some place out of the way to sleep. "I think we should try to find a place inside. I don't think there will be an attack tonight but we should be out of the way just in case."

Both Winona and her mother nodded. They ventured into the stone house to find a space of unoccupied floor to sleep. Seeing no room on the main floor, and reluctant to go into the cellar, they started back out, one woman called out and said they could probably find room upstairs. Margaret wanted to kiss her. She felt so unwelcome here. Others did not share this woman's kindness. Their hostile eyes followed Winona as she walked in between Margaret and Mother to the steep stairs.

The rooms were uncrowded comparatively speaking to the first floor. Many of the windows were broken so fresh air spilled in. For some reason, this made Margaret feel better. The first floor had been very stuffy. After four nights out in the open, she wasn't sure she could sleep in a cooped-up room for the night. Still the stone walls were nice and thick, bullets could not go through a stone wall. Margaret felt safe. Had it not been for all the noises made by everyone else, she might have slept better, believing the stone would protect them.

Chapter 17

Scavenging New Ulm

THE MORNING STARTED PEACEFULLY ENOUGH. They were allowed to visit the outhouse and forage for food. The town was running out of supplies. The kindly woman from last night suggested that Margaret and Winona walk through the town finding what they could for a breakfast. Again, Margaret was struck by how hostile so many of the women were. Very few spoke to them, which was understandable with how tense everyone was. But the anger in their eyes towards Winona upset Margaret very much.

Winona had not killed anyone. Her friend had not done anything wrong. In fact she should be with her own family but had chosen to save Margaret and her family instead. Somehow Margaret knew that her words would fall on deaf ears. Hate poisoned the mind and would not allow people to hear the truth. They had baby Isaac with them and a large basket. Look in any house they were told. Try and find any food that might have been over looked earlier.

It was frightening to go into empty houses. Margaret and Winona worked quickly in each one, checking the Hoosier cabinets and under the dry sinks for food. Some kitchens had a cellar door under the kitchen table. Most were out of food, the open doors showing they had already been raided. The Hoosier cabinets were empty of flour and sugar.

Finally, they had success, a root cellar with fresh vegetables. They filled their basket and Margaret's apron with potatoes, onions, carrots, and sausage. There was so much, they needed to make two trips. The kindly lady thanked them profusely. Her name was Anna, and she seemed to be in charge of the cooking and feeding of the town. Many of the other women were too busy to stop and say thanks. They chopped firewood into kindling, got the fires going, and hauled water to get a soup started.

Women were everywhere, many working but some refusing to leave the stone homes they had sheltered in, too afraid to come out and get food started. Margaret wondered if they might dash out when the soup was ready to eat.

Most of the men remained in firing positions behind the barricades. They had hastily erected firing pits around the center of town. The girls were able to walk through this barricade a few more times, bringing back all the food from the kitchen cellar. As the soup started to simmer and there was less work to do, more women took time to shoot burning glares at Winona. After cleaning out the cellar and dropping all the food at the makeshift kitchen, Margaret decided enough was enough.

"It's the moccasins." Margaret announced. "We need to get you a pair of good German boots." She doubted it would be enough, but it felt better to have a purpose and leave the glares while the soup was cooking. *Perhaps I should look for a bonnet too. I hate wearing them but now that I've experienced a sunburn, it might not hurt to keep that from happening again. Plus a bonnet might help hide Winona's face.*

Finding a dry goods store, they bumped into the owner as he was heading out. Surprised to see a man not in the pits or by the barricade, Margaret asked if he had any shoes to spare.

"Shoes? Aren't you supposed to be looking for food? There's no food in here, I was just looking for some. Shoes, why shoes?" The owner looked at them and sneered, "And what will you be paying with?" Then he shrugged and sighed, "It is probably better to let a couple of half-breeds have them for free than let them be burned or looted by the complete savages."

Going back into the store, he told them to be quick about it, as he was needed at the barricades. He let them try on ready-made shoes until they each had a pair that fit. Then in a surprisingly nice gesture, he gave them both fine, machine-made stockings too.

Margaret had never owned a pair of stockings so nice. Winona enjoyed the softness of the stockings but didn't like how hot they were and complained how awkwardly the shoes made her walk. The owner of the store still had a lot of stock. He said he had come to see if there were any dry crackers in the back of his counter but he couldn't find any. He asked them to look to see if there was anything to eat and to close the door on their way out.

The girls left Isaac on the floor where they had set him while they tried on shoes, and wandered through the store. There was cloth, and ribbons, and panes of glass, but not much in the way of anything edible. They dug behind the counter and were finally rewarded with a tin of crackers and a small jar of pickles. No bonnets, for which Winona voiced her gratitude. Taking the crackers and pickles, they picked up Isaac and started back to the center of town.

Fortunately it was only a block or so, as Winona complained the whole way. She had tucked her moccasins into the shawl she used to tie Isaac to her waist. Winona complained of the stiffness of the shoes, and how hard it would be to run in this get-up. Margaret let her whine a little.

After dropping off their edibles at the cooking station, they rested by the side of the house. Margaret's mother brought over two plates of soup, same as yesterday. She looked wan and pale but her energy was strong. After breakfast and clean up, Mother found a shady side of the house and lay down to rest with Isaac. The glares from the women proved to be too much and drove Winona and Margaret to continue scavenging for food.

During their mid-morning scavenging, they found more root vegetables and bags and bags of flour. One of the women let out a huzzah when she saw the flour. Bread, she yelled as she led them to the bakery. The oven had not even had a fire lit in it, as the town had thought it had used all of its flour the night before. By noon, all the bags had been brought to the bakery and loaves were rising and baking. As each batch came out, the men gathered in small shifts to eat and have a mug of beer. Then they returned to duty and another batch of men came to eat.

The young children were allowed to eat with their fathers, while the women and older girls ate after all the men had eaten. After Winona and Margaret ate bread and more soup, they walked towards a different part of town, scavenging for food was something they did very well! Passing the barricades and rifle-fire pits, Margaret didn't think they looked very strong or defendable. The men were digging and piling. The two girls were told by both bossy men and women alike to stay out of their way. The town's defenders looked ragged, sleep worn but very determined.

Margaret noticed a fair number of mixed bloods like Joseph, just as yesterday. Their plan for Winona might work if she could pretend to be mixed. Margaret was thankful that Winona had chosen to help her and mother. She wanted to help ease Winona's pain over the looks and hatred she was getting.

The men were not giving them the same looks of hatred. Margaret wondered why that was? At least Winona did not have to make the decision the men had to make. They were firing on their friends and relatives. Winona had been saved that decision by being a girl. Perhaps since the mixed-blood men had chosen to join the whites, the women knew where their loyalties lay. Could they not make the same decision about Winona? Realizing that by her being here, she had helped a white family and made a tough decision as well?

If they survived this turmoil, what would happen to all of them? If the whites won, what would happen to those who were part Dakota? Would they be welcomed back into Dakota families? The Minnesotans might wish to drive all Dakota from the land as punishment for the war? Would the mixed-bloods be allowed to stay? Those who had helped? Like Winona? Like Joseph?

If the Dakota won. Could the Dakota win? If they somehow managed it, would Joseph and Winona ever visit their families again? Margaret worried about her friend, perhaps so she didn't have to think about their immediate situation or her own future.

Chapter 18

Attack on New Ulm

WINONA AND MARGARET DID NOT SCRAMBLE with the other women into the stone houses and the cellars as soon as the first plumes of smoke appeared on the horizon. They watched from behind the barricade. The smoke grew closer. They could see the smoke was from many small fires not a large one. The Dakota were burning the haystacks the girls had passed yesterday.

Winona had tried to tell some of the men that the Dakota would try to draw them out of their barricades. She, of course, had been told to go away and leave them alone. Margaret and Winona had been able to find Joseph, and Winona had whispered her fear to him that the Dakota would try taunting the townsmen. Hoping to draw them out from their well-defended position.

Joseph listened to her and reassured both girls. He said the town's defenders had not fallen for that tactic the day before and he felt sure that the commander of the town, Colonel Flandreau, was going to stick to his plan of defending this center only. Colonel Flandreau knew the Dakota warriors would try to burn the outer buildings to create a smoke screen. The smoke would hide them as they advanced towards the town's defenses.

Joseph said the colonel had things well set up. He showed Winona and Margaret how the younger men, boys really, would run ammunition to the men in the rifle pits so they could keep a steady fire at all times. The barricade formed a circle or square really, and this would make it impossible for the Dakota to break through.

Joseph shared Winona's fear that the Dakota would attempt to draw out the defenders and then a second group of Dakota would attack the town while the men were out on the prairie. The Dakota had the advantage on the prairie. The settlers had the advantage in the town. Joseph said the commander knew this and that she should go back into the center of town, the stone building. It would be safer there. He gave her and Margaret a wan smile and a friendly shove back to the center, before turning his eyes back to the plumes of smoke on the horizon.

"At least he didn't pat me on the head," Winona said as they turned to go back to the stone building with Margaret.

"No," Margaret agreed. "He seemed to really listen to you."

When they got to the stone house, they noticed there were no other women outside. All the women were already inside. Great piles of hoop skirts rested by the door.

"To make more room," Margaret told Winona. "They will be all trying to fit into the large cellar underneath. Mother has not worn her hoops since we left the house. She has no worries about anyone seeing her without them now!" Winona permitted herself a wry grin as Margaret pulled her into the house.

They paused at the door to look out one more time, and were promptly scolded loudly. They froze. A loud woman told them of the girl who had died during the last attack. "She too had wanted a better look and wouldn't listen to any of us. Called us old biddies, she did. Where is she now, you might wonder? She's dead. A bullet killed her right where you're standing now. Will you be defying your elders too? Get inside now. There's room still in the cellar."

Margaret and Winona quickly stepped further inside, they certainly did not want to get shot. They had already seen enough of the effects of this war. They worked their way to the ladder and went down to join the safety of the thick cellar.

As Margaret lowered herself down the ladder, she could feel the smell of fear and perspiration thicken the air. It seemed as if she were breathing in a poisonous vapor of terror, hatred, fear, and revenge. There seemed few if any hopeful thoughts in this noxious brew.

She waited for her eyes to adjust. The light was so dim. Due to the risk of fire, only a few pierced tin barn lanterns were lit. Winona followed Margaret carefully over to where her mother was. The three of them huddled together, with baby Isaac. They had survived so far, mostly due to Winona's planning, clever thinking, and her knowledge. They had done this all by themselves. Now, though, it was up to someone else to keep her family safe. This made Margaret feel weak, as if she were not in charge of herself.

To Winona the day seemed to go on forever. She fought against the almost overpowering urge to run. What would running get her? Either side would mistake her for the other and she would be killed. Still it was awful sitting here in the almost dark listening to the muffled sounds of battle, the noise of bullets and glass shattering.

The noises made the women more anxious and fearful. They clutched at their children. The older ones moaned in fear, and the babies cried and wailed. There wasn't any way to keep them all quiet. No room to pace, or even sway them back to sleep. The air seemed to grow thicker. Winona panicked. What if they all suffocated down here? Safe from the bullets, but dead anyway.

The thought scared her so much that she could not get it out of her brain. She leaped up, but Margaret pulled her down, once, twice, three times. "Do you want to get yourself killed?" she yelled in her ear.

Winona tried to focus on the words and sounds around her. The infants wailed, and the Germans muttered. "*Mein Gott, mein*

Gott, mein Gott!" That was all she could hear. Winona could not tell whether they were cursing, praying or simply speaking. She could hear the men yelling at each other and this made the women quiet as they tried to decipher what the men were saying and whether it was their husband, brother, or father speaking.

The noise of the battle raged. The Dakota were fighting hard. Winona could hear how the battle moved around the barricades. Sometimes the noises of gunfire seemed muffled as if the fighting was across town from where they were. Other times it sounded directly overhead.

The townsmen were fighting back hard, not allowing the Dakota to find a weak spot. The discipline of the townsmen was impressive from what Winona could hear. They were not being drawn out, nor were they rushing into gaps. Steady fire, pushing each Dakota advance back, time and time again.

Sometimes, there would be long pauses when the only words the women could hear were, "*Wasser, bitte*" or "*Wir brauchen munitions schnell*" from the men on the lines. Young boys were running ammunition and water to the men. Winona wished she could have done that. Perhaps she should have argued with Margaret's mother for a pair of britches instead of a dress.

She smelled smoke, and the air grew even thicker. She coughed as did the rest of the women but none dared to go up and Winona knew she would be yelled at if she tried. Somehow the fear of white woman yelling at her was worse than her fear of bullets. It had grown quiet for a very long time. The occasional shot, the occasional shout. But silence, a silence filled with smoke.

Then a great huzzah went through the town. The women stood, hugged each other and started clambered up to the street. Winona was hugged repeatedly by women she was sure would have killed her yesterday, or even offered her up as a sacrifice earlier today.

Margaret climbed up first and then reached down as her mother handed up Isaac, before she and Winona scrambled up and out. They stumbled out into an eerie landscape of smoke and haze. It was less claustrophobic, but the smoke in the air still made them cough and their eyes tear up. Almost all the buildings had burned except the handful in the middle. Turning slowly in a circle, Winona could see burning buildings everywhere she looked.

But the town had made it through alive. The Dakota had not taken it, although not much seemed to be left. Hundreds of buildings had been destroyed. Colonel Flandreau would not release the men from their positions. But he did say the women could start on an evening meal.

He asked the young girls to form bucket brigades from the pump and hand water to the men to put out the closest fires to the barricade. They needed the buildings that were left and their barricades were made largely of furniture and pieces of firewood. Winona eagerly took a place in line. Work, action—this would help her to stop thinking. To stop worrying about what was next. She was the closest to the barricades, Margaret next to her. Baby Isaac lay on a shawl by the other babies next to where the mothers were preparing a meal. Was it really an evening meal? Could it be the middle of the day still? Had the attack lasted only hours? Winona could not see the sun. There was too much smoke in the air obscuring it. The fires gave everything a reddish glow. It felt as if it were twilight, but Winona did not know.

Chapter 19

New Ulm Must Be Abandoned

MARGARET HANDED FULL BUCKETS of water to Winona and empty ones back as fast as she could. The line moved in a circle pivoting out from its center, the pump, to squelch the blazes all along the barricade. After what felt like hours, they were told they could stop. Margaret could not tell when the smoky daylight had turned over to the full dark of a summer's moonless night. Smoke still lay that thick. Fires still burned in the outskirts of New Ulm, but Colonel Flandreau said it was too risky to deal with those.

They could eat and rest. Margaret dropped her bucket by the pump and wandered over to the cook pots. The women were ladling large scoops of potato and onion soup on tin plates. The men ate first, but somehow the girls of the bucket brigade found themselves getting served right along with them. As soon as they were finished, they brought their plates to get washed, so they could be used by the next people in line.

The barrels of beer were almost all gone, but each man and boy got at least a mug if he wanted. Margaret didn't care for the taste of beer. She filled her mug with water and drank two mugs full before handing it to Winona.

Gone were the looks of hatred directed at Winona. Everyone was relieved to be alive and exhausted. The women finally ate, giving seconds to the younger children. Margaret saw their loss in their eyes. She knew that the children who had survived would become the mother's lifeline to a future.

The town waited for another attack. Colonel Flandreau posted guards, but most of the mixed-blood men as well as Winona told him that Dakota did not fight at night. All spent an uneasy night. Exhausted, yet unable to sleep, Margaret shifted her body to a more comfortable position, wishing she could as easily shift her mind to easier thoughts than what would happen tomorrow.

The next day was tense with waiting. Winona and Margaret salvaged what food could be found, but, even ranging further out from the center of town than they had before, they found few kitchen cellars with food. Too many buildings had gone up in smoke. The remains of the burned out homes were too unsafe to enter. Plus any food in a cellar would have been ruined in the heat from the fire.

Food was getting dangerously short. More men from the countryside came to defend the town, which was welcome, but many came with a family member or two. More mouths to feed. Everyone soon realized how low their supplies were. Word spread through the town's center that Colonel Flandreau had ordered the town evacuated. They would travel in the remaining wagons, under guard, to Mankato. No baggage, only people and bedding.

Margaret wondered if their tin pail counted as baggage? She hoped not. It was all they had.

Winona was appalled at how much the townspeople were taking, even with the colonel's order to leave everything behind. Where had it all come from? Boxes and baggage, piles and piles of them. So few buildings were left. Where had they found it all? Yet she sympathized with their desire to bring what they could with them. It was all they had left, and they were reluctant to leave anything behind. Winona understood this as she fingered her knife. What did she have left? A pair of moccasins? Two blue ribbons, soiled and torn, an extra pair of stockings?

Yet as she watched the piles of goods mount on the wagons, she wondered at the excess. So many clothes, shoes, blankets, and bedding. Why so much? It would be worth nothing if they were attacked? Plus, all of this would slow the wagons down. It was already slowing the entire process of loading the wagons.

Winona looked at their tin pail and glanced at Margaret. Margaret grinned a fiendish grin. "You don't have to be so happy about how ridiculous I look!" Winona hissed at her friend. Somehow, as the townspeople raided their destroyed and half destroyed homes in search of bedding and changes of clothes, they had found bonnets for Margaret, her mother, and Winona.

For the first time in her life, Winona was wearing a bonnet, at Margaret's mother's insistence. Margaret and her mother knew that Winona had saved their lives. To repay her they were making her wear a big ugly bonnet. Some thanks.

Finally, the wagons were lined up and loaded up, and the horses were brought from the stables and hitched to pull them. Men who were not loading or hitching seemed to be gathered in the center, arguing around a big barrel. Winona wandered over to listen to what they were saying. It was the kind of barrel that usually held whiskey. There were words painted on it, but they did not say whiskey. Whiskey was one of the words Winona had learned how to spell well as it was always distributed at the lodge meetings and annuity meetings.

Winona asked Margaret what they were painting on the barrel. Margaret read aloud, "It says gift."

"Gift?" Winona questioned. "What kind of a gift comes in a barrel?"

"No, you don't understand. *Gift* is poison in German. The men are leaving a barrel of poison here. They hope the braves will drink it, but they want to make sure no German drinks it, so they are labeling it with a warning in German!"

Margaret looked at Winona with a look of horror. The townsmen were doing something that seemed worse than anything already done in this time of terror. Leaving poison out for one's enemies? This would mean the warriors would not die in honor in battle but by drinking what they thought was the white man's liquor. Little Crow always called it devil water. Perhaps he was truly correct. It would be the death of them.

Winona watched Colonel Flandreau come by and order a stop to it. He told the men in a very quiet voice that this was wrong, then ordered that the barrel smashed.

The front wagons finally started moving out in a long guarded column. There were so many people in the town. It would take a long time for all these wagons to get going. It seemed as if there were over one hundred of them, and more people than Margaret thought possible. Many women and children had come out of cellars, for the first time in three days. Margaret did not want to think what it would smell like in those cellars.

Some folks had arrived yesterday and many more were pouring into the town even as they were leaving it. All were told they had to follow the wagons for their safety.

Winona likened their situation to a hot summer wind blowing on the prairie. The grass stalks bent in waves, one after another. Only the winds blowing now spread fire with them, death and destruction. To stop and rest risked the winds catching up with them, risked their being consumed by fire. When would the destruction stop? When would he settlers reach safety? Would they arrive in Mankato, only to be told they would not be safe until they had reached Saint Paul?

The town's defenders and any who could walked beside the wagons. Margaret's mother rode in a wagon with some of the wounded. Baby Isaac had gotten quiet again after the last two days of confined spaces and smoky air. Winona could not blame him. She had no desire to talk herself. She and Margaret walked.

Joseph came alongside to walk with Winona and Margaret. Winona felt safer with him near. He actually had seemed to listen to her concerns that the town's defenders would get tricked into fighting on the prairie or try to put out fires on the edge of town. He gave her a half grin when he saw her bonnet. Again, she brooded at the injustice of having to wear the ridiculous thing.

The noise the caravan made sounded like thunder. So many plodding horses, so many squeaking wheels and tromping feet. She knew she should feel safe with so many people, so many men with guns. But she did not.

For days, she and Margaret had silently slunk through the prairie. Now to walk so in the open with so many made her feel like an easy target. The caravan did not stop for food or any breaks. Few spoke. Most climbed in wagons to rest, climbed out again a little later so another could take his rest. Children sometimes cried and occasionally a women wept. To Winona the sounds were a hushed agony. Quiet whimpers, scared whispers. It felt as if everyone shared her fears. They scanned the horizon. They hoped not to be attacked.

The prairie was so open. So vulnerable. Mankato would be safe. They all thought this. Mankato would be safe.

Margaret could tell that Winona was having the same thoughts as she. They had thought New Ulm would be safe. It was not. Would Mankato be attacked as they arrived? Would they need to flee to another town? To Saint Paul? Where would it be safe?

It was almost thirty miles to Mankato, and Margaret could feel every mile of it. The walk was endless. The sun scorched and the heat shimmered the air. It was hard to keep going, impossible to stop.

The land was undamaged here. No homes had been destroyed. Barns and haystacks still stood. Corn and oats ripened in the fields. Occasionally a cow mooed. This gave Margaret hope that they might walk out of the war, put it behind them.

Water was distributed along the way. Colonel Flandreau had packed wagons with barrels of it. Margaret used the dipper and drank, and then she dampened part of her shawl to wipe her face and Isaac's. She handed Mother the dipper. Mother drank but did not respond to Margaret's questions of whether she was all right.

Margaret's legs ached but riding in the wagon did not alleviate the pain. She held on to Winona's hand for support. They shared their tiredness together. Mother's eyes had dulled. She held Isaac but stared out onto the prairie. She had heard other women tell of their families being killed in front of them. As more and more women shared their stories, Margaret realized her mother knew that Pa was dead. It wasn't an unknown, a question anymore. Mother could not hope that he might still be alive. For once in her life, Margaret was thankful for the bonnet she wore. At least, it hid her eyes from others.

Chapter 20

Arrival in Mankato

THEY REACHED MANKATO as the sun set. The sunset bathed the prairie in red light. Just like the light from a fire, Margaret thought. It seemed as if the entire town had gathered to meet the refugees. It was overwhelming to be stared at by so many. Margaret felt like a curiosity from the circus. She was just like them. *Or perhaps I'm not. I have been through a war, a battle. They have not. We all share the same hope that it will not come here to Mankato.*

Many of the Mankato folks carried blankets and food. They offered their homes. They offered their stables. The men started to unhitch the horses, and Mankato women started leading off groups of New Ulm women and children.

The wagons with wounded were brought to makeshift hospitals like those they had abandoned. The hotel was turned into a hospital, and the townsfolk of Mankato helped unload the wounded men, and a few women.

Margaret felt like crying. Seeing so many strangers open their homes, hearts, and arms to them. Many settlers confided to each other that they had to go further east, although they would rest in Mankato. They planned to head to St. Paul or even more eastern cities where they had relatives who could shelter them. So many wished to leave behind the sights and sounds they had witnessed. Many still feared the Dakota would attack.

Mankato had heard rumors of attacks being made by the other tribes. Even as the New Ulm survivors had been winding their way through the prairie, stories circulated that the Winnebago tribes were attacking whites. Some men had left Mankato to defend Blue Earth County. Some shared their fears that the Ojibway would attack as well, and if all the native people worked together, even Saint Paul would not be strong enough to protect their lives.

Margaret had listened to this talk but did not put much worry into those stories. From what Winona had said, the Dakota liked working individually. She could not imagine the tribes banding together in the way the settlers suggested. They were talking out of fear. Still, that old terror washed over her, alternating with waves of relief. They had not been attacked on the prairie. They were thirty miles away from New Ulm.

Perhaps they were safe. Relief seeped through her and replaced terror with exhaustion. Margaret sagged against the wagon that her mother was still in. Her mother was struggling to get her bearings. The wounded had been unloaded, and she needed to get out of the wagon before the man driving it took it to find stables, water, and hay for the horses.

Margaret reached over the side panel of wood and took Baby Isaac from her. Then, handing Isaac to Winona, she helped her mother down out of the wagon. Winona continued to hold Isaac. Margaret saw Winona glance around, but the looks of hatred that had greeted them when they reached New Ulm, were not present here. Mankato had not been attacked, the townspeople here had heard about what was happening but had not seen it for themselves. Their loved ones had not been killed in front of them.

Margaret stood with an arm around her mother, next to Winona and wondered what they should do. Somehow their tin pail was still with them. The nappies could be called clean but that was not a completely true statement for such a strong-smelling bucket. They stared around themselves for a while wondering what they should do.

Margaret felt overwhelmed. There were so many people. Yet it was eerily quiet. Many spoke in hushed tones and even the children were subdued and seldom spoke.

Margaret started to ask Winona what they should do, but she was interrupted. A woman dressed all in black came and hugged Margaret's mother as if she knew her well. Margaret knew they had no family in Mankato so she wondered who this woman was. She did not have to wonder for long.

The woman in black started talking immediately and continued to hug Margaret's mother. Then she hugged Margaret. Then Winona. Talking all the while. Before they knew it, they were being herded down the street by this woman, the Widow Shaw she called herself. She continued to carry on a one-sided conversation punctuated with friendly nods to everyone they passed along the way.

Margaret's mother attempted to talk, but the Widow Shaw's tongue ran right over her words. She held Mother's hand the entire walk to her house. Margaret found herself soothed by the widow's rambling. She let the words flow over her like a balm, or the rainy days of peace they had experienced on the prairie. The widow's words were like that rain, soft and kind, hiding the hurt. Making it seem softer and less painful.

"Oh, you poor things. What you've been through I can't even imagine. The newspaper has been describing things something terrible. But you don't want to talk about that right now. No, no. What you need is supper, a bath, and bed, in that order. Then we will figure out what's your next step should be. I live alone in this big rambling house, so you can just come along with me, and we'll get you sorted out. You'll feel so much better after a bath and a good supper in your belly. A good night's sleep too. Yes indeed, you will feel better in the morning and be able to think straight once all the prairie dust is off of you. You'll feel right as rain come morning, I dare say. I have such a big house with lots of room for the children Mr. Shaw and I thought would come along after our marriage, but they didn't happen to come along. Now I live alone, as the good Mister Shaw passed on almost three years ago.

She didn't seem to mind that no one spoke but she, didn't seem to need them to add to the conversation. "He just went to bed one night and I plum couldn't get him to wake up the next morning. Feel mighty bad about it too as I was in the middle of giving him a good scolding about being a good-for-nothing laze about. Imagine my chagrin when there he was gone off to his just reward with my scolding the last thing he might of heard!"

The Widow Shaw pulled in a sharp intake of breath. "Oh my goodness what am I yammering on about. Death is not something I should be discussing right now. Not with all that you've seen. What I meant to say was that you'll stay with me for as long as it takes to get your feet back under you again. The house is big enough for all of us, me living there all by myself isn't natural like."

On and on she prattled. Margaret listened to some of it and let some of it just pass her by. The town looked so unnatural to her. It was all clean and well ordered. Nothing had been burned, and the people stared at her with a natural curiosity. It seemed confusing to have this part of the land so untouched by war and to have devastation so complete a few miles away. This must be how a soldier felt when he returns home from battle. As if he could not believe how good the rest of the world still was.

Margaret wondered if soldiers carried anger or resentment with them about that. She felt it was somehow wrong for so many people to be just fine and for her family to have lost so much. Here in Mankato, people still had their homes, their clothes, and their obnoxious big brothers. She did not have any of that left. Before she allowed herself to wallow completely in self-pity, she asked the widow what news she had heard. "Where are the soldiers from Fort Snelling? Did the Dakota attack elsewhere besides the Lower Agency, Fort Ridgley, and New Ulm?"

"Oh, my dear," the Widow Shaw said. "All we know is what's in the newspapers, and it's so hard to tell what's true and what isn't. One wonders if all of it could be true? Sibly is leading the soldiers from Fort Snelling. The governor himself appointed him. So many of those brave men were all ready to head off to fight those southern rebels and now, they have to turn around and head back into the prairie to fight the Dakota and save their own homes! Tsk, tsk. What a soldier must think when his orders change like that. I suppose most of them aren't much more than farm boys getting ready to be soldiers. We just had a parade a few days before all this started and sent off some of the finest young men you'll ever see to rid this nation of the hateful scourge of slavery. Our country will be whole again, and free!

Margaret had turned away. As awful as slavery seemed, it had been overtaken in her mind by the war at hand.

"Oh, would you listen to me prattle on," the Widow Shaw said. "Talking about war and battles again. I must confess I'm as nervous as a cat in a room full of rocking chairs, terrified I'll say the wrong thing to you, and here I've managed to say all the wrong things anyway. Well, here we are. Let's get you in. I've got a nice copper tub in the kitchen all ready, and water warming for bathing. The stew's ready and biscuits too. I even kept a kettle on the stove for some tea while you take turns bathing."

Chapter 21

The Widow Shaw's Place

WINONA WAS NOT LISTENING to the Widow Shaw, but it took effort to do this. The woman would not stop talking even as she got them into her home and showed them where they could take a bath. In the kitchen with water warmed on the stove and food steaming on the table, Winona and Margaret bathed first while Margaret's mother ate and had tea, and then each put on some voluminous nightgown of the widow's. To Winona, this was far worse than the bonnet.

Winona tied her knife back into its place on her thigh and her leather bag to her waist under the nightgown. Both girls made a neat stack of their clothing on the porch. The widow said they would do laundry and air things out first thing in the morning. The widow showed Winona and Margaret where to dump the bath water and then sent them to the parlor.

They sat in the plush parlor while Margaret's mother bathed Isaac and then herself. Then the Widow Shaw brought more food, a cold supper of ham and sliced bread. Margaret started yawning halfway through her second meal, which encouraged a fresh round of, "You must be so exhausted," from the Widow Shaw.

Before Winona could even blink she found herself tucked into a soft, warm bed with Margaret and being kissed on the forehead both by Margaret's mother and the Widow Shaw, who led Margaret's mother out and to another room.

As the Widow Shaw closed the door, Winona could hear her prattling on down the hall. "Oh, those poor dears, and you too. What you've seen and experienced! No, now you don't need to say a word. Let's find that cradle I stored in the attic after I realized the Good Lord wasn't sending us any children. Baby Isaac will be fit as a fiddle in it, and you need the rest too my dear."

Margaret's mother murmured something as she followed the widow up to the attic but the words were lost to Winona. Leaning over, Winona whispered in Margaret's ear. "I bet she talks in her sleep too!"

Margaret chuckled and then sighed happily, burying her nose in the sheets and quilts. She seemed blissfully content to be in a nightgown and underneath what felt like forty blankets on such a hot night.

Winona, however, found it stifling. The nightdress seemed to be in cahoots with the sheets to pull her under the blankets and suffocate her. Margaret had already fallen asleep. But Winona could not drift off.

Finally Winona thrust the covers aside and got up to see if she could find a place on the porch. This way she could watch the night stars. Holding the nightgown up off the floor in one hand so she wouldn't trip, she inched her way down the stairs. On her way to the porch, she overheard the widow and Margaret's mother talking in low voices, and she thought it best not to disturb them.

She quietly slunk back into the room where Margaret was snoring. A fact Winona would be delighted to tell her in the morning. Opening the window to let in some air, she rolled herself in a blanket. Making sure she was near the window to watch the stars, Winona finally fell asleep on the floor.

When she awoke, her brain was consumed with plans and thoughts of how to get back to her band and family. *Perhaps I should have left before they all started to Mankato? Everyone was so busy. I could have snuck off then. But I didn't even think of escaping, I was so busy loading and helping. Plus I was scared of another attack. Staying with Margaret and keeping her safe was more important. Still,* Winona sighed, *what am I to do now?*

Mankato seemed safe. As safe a place as she could find, for Margaret and her mother. With them taken care of by the chatty Widow Shaw, now seemed like a good time to get back to the reservation and find her family. Winona had not meant for her separation to be so long.

One thing had led to another, each the right thing to do at the time. But it all had led her further and further from her own loved ones. Perhaps she had been too hard on Brown Wing. He had made a decision in the moment of what to do. But then his decision had far greater consequences than he realized. No, Winona was not like Brown Wing. She had thought to warn her friend. He had thought of his wounded pride.

Well, it didn't matter how I got here. The point is to find a way to get back. Here I am almost a week after I warned my friend of danger, in a house run by the chattiest woman on earth, in Mankato. I am further away from home than I have ever been in my life. I have to get back. My family might leave without me if the soldiers push them west. Father would never surrender. He will keep fighting even if it looks as if the Dakota will lose all.

She knew she needed a plan. Winona was grinding her teeth and clenching the handle of her knife. She had not gotten up yet. Margaret was still asleep, and she needed the thinking time. *I'll tell Margaret I'm leaving. She and I can walk to the outskirts of town together. There, I'll give Margaret back the dress and shawls. Then I'll run all the way home.*

Just the thought of running soothed Winona. She got up and peered out the window. It was a perfect day. There was sunshine and light dancing clouds. Winona could not wait to get started. It was what she had to do.

Margaret woke in the morning and felt as if she had never slept better. Winona was at the window looking as if she were a caged bird. They spent the morning indulging in the largest breakfast they had ever eaten and then getting fitted into some of the widow's "old" clothes. Winona kept trying to get to the back porch, but the widow kept a keen eye on her. The widow kept both girls so busy all morning that it was not until after lunch that they had the chance to be alone in each other's company.

Margaret's mother was so handy with her needlework. She had altered two dresses of the Widow Shaw's. Held together mostly with big basting stitches, the widow and Margaret's mother still agreed they were "decent enough" to go out in public.

Both Margaret and Winona eagerly escaped the house though the front door. They left the widow prattling on to Mother about "what fine seamstress skills she had. And have you thought of opening your own shop?"

Winona started outlining her plan to Margaret the second they were in the front yard. They walked as she explained what she had to do. "I plan on getting back into my own clothes and moccasins, then dandy myself up with one of your impossible dresses. Will you walk with me to the outskirts of town? From there I'll follow the river and run back to my band."

Margaret did not have any valid reason to hold her in Mankato but she voiced her objection of Winona's safety. "You can't just wander around the prairie dressed like a white woman. What if the soldiers shoot first, thinking you're a spy? Don't you remember reading about those Revolutionary spies in our schoolbooks? It wasn't pretty how they got taken care of! People are so jumpy around here, they're liable to shoot first and ask questions later! What if the Dakota shoot you for wearing white clothes? What if you can't find your family or Red Middle Voice's band? You said yourself; they won't be where you left them. What if you have to wander alone for weeks on the prairie, every day fearing for your life if found by the wrong people? What if the entire tribe left the state? You would never catch up with them?"

Margaret stopped to take in a big breath and then started on her tirade again. "Wouldn't it be better to wait and find out where Little Crow is so at least you could go in the right direction? Perhaps we should go find Joseph to help? A little more information could save your life. Besides," Margaret laid out her final piece of information like one would lay the winning card in a hand of poker. "Getting your clothes isn't going to happen. The widow burned your clothes, ours too, worried about disease."

Chapter 22

Winona Is Trapped

WINONA LISTENED TO THIS LAST STATEMENT in absolute shock. It was as if she could see the door of a cage slamming shut in front of her. Her plans to get to the prairie and run home were dashed. She couldn't run in a white lady's dress. She had uncovered the real reason white ladies didn't run and now there was no one Dakota to share this fact with.

Winona knew deep in her heart it would be better to wait and find some answers before blindly running out into the prairie dressed like a white woman. But she yearned to run. She needed to run. She could feel her legs trying to pull her out of Mankato and out on to the prairie. She had missed her chance to freedom. She should have left Margaret and her mother when they started on the trek to Mankato but she couldn't bear the uncertainty of their getting attacked on the prairie before reaching safety. She agreed to find out more information if they went immediately to find Joseph.

Margaret agreed, and they went to the center of town to find anyone who might know what had happened to the soldiers that had escorted them to Mankato.

Margaret and Winona did not have much luck in gaining any answers to their questions that day. The soldiers were under the command of Colonel Flandreau. He had ordered barricades and trenches to be built around Mankato. He had them far out of town so the townsmen could fall back into town if necessary and defend from a second line. They did not have time to pause in their work to answer questions from two pesky girls. "You'd be home, if you knew what was good for you!" was the response they most often received to their search for Joseph or the colonel.

They walked home defeated. The house was downright cheerful. Baby Isaac was babbling. Mother was smiling. Of course, the Widow Shaw was talking. They had a supper and then spent time in the parlor discussing the latest news. Very little of it felt like news. Most was rumor and gossip. Still Winona and Margaret hung on every word. The soldiers were on their way from Fort Snelling. They were moving slowly. "How long does it take to cover the miles?" Winona asked Margaret. Margaret shrugged.

"Not as long as they are taking," the widow replied. She had sharp ears, when she wanted to. "Sibley must be hoping the fight will be out of the Indians by the time he gets here. It's not right though. Innocents dead, and he takes his sweet time."

The next morning both girls left after breakfast to find Joseph or the colonel. However, neither was ever where they were supposed to be. Margaret and Winona spent several fruitless days trying to track him down. They started each day at the defense works west of town. The walk was long. Colonel Flandreau did not want Mankato destroyed as New Ulm had been. He planned to keep the fight west of town, if the Dakota came here.

Winona changed into her moccasins each day once they were out of sight of townpeople's eyes. The widow had not burned them, claiming they were too beautiful to burn. Winona was very grateful. She could almost forgive the widow for burning her short-dress and leather leggings. Almost. Margaret helped her cut slits in the new dress and petticoat combination, so Winona could access her knife. She kept her bag at her waist as well. Always ready. Always hoping to run, but as the days passed, she started to worry that she had left it too long already.

Margaret could tell Winona was getting more and more fretful each day. She rubbed the handle of her knife. She ground her teeth both sleeping and awake. It was more than Margaret could bear. Margaret knew Winona needed to get back to her own mother, but she knew that information from the colonel or Joseph could mean the difference between her friend living or dieing.
If only they could find the colonel? Or find anyone who knew what was going on? The colonel was always busy somewhere, and they never seemed to see Joseph. Finally due to their persistence, or annoyance, they were granted an "audience" with Colonel Flandreau.

Although he only gave them two minutes of his time, he did tell them that the Dakota were still attacking. There was vicious fighting at Birch Coulee. The Dakota had crushed soldiers from Fort Snelling. "Just like Taoyateduta said!" Winona burst out.

"Yes, indeed." Colonel Flandreau gave them both a penetrating stare before continuing. "The soldiers and the New Ulm defenders were almost wiped out. We have more reports that Fort Abercrombie, very far to the north and along the Red River has been surrounded. The fort may still be without water or food. Has been for weeks. Forest City's been attacked. Hutchinson too. The Dakota seem to be attacking everywhere. There's no possible way you can leave. I don't believe the Dakota can win though. I believe we'll push them back. But right now they are winning. This war is not over.

"I need to keep building fortifications here and around the other towns and forts. Governor Ramsey has ordered this. I don't think the Dakota have it in them to spread this far east. Girls, you're safe here. Out on the prairie is another story."

The colonel paused again and looked hard at Winona. "Here, take this, Winona. It might save your life. One of my men told me what you did for your friends. This makes it official." He handed Winona a piece of paper folded in half. Then he walked away.

The girls were dismissed. Disheartened they continued to search for Joseph. However, a sergeant informed them that many of the mixed-bloods had gone to join Sibley at his headquarters in Fort Ridgley. Taking Colonel Flandreau's advice, the girls felt they had to wait. It was all they could do.

Winona fumed when the colonel spoke about them not being allowed to leave the town. How could they be stopped truly? It would be an easy task to sneak out one evening, or even in broad daylight. She and Margaret had been leaving the town every day for the past week trying to speak to this high and mighty colonel and had not once been stopped. She ranted and raved about this idiot of a man the entire walk back to the Widow Shaw's house.

"What did he give you?" Margaret asked. Winona looked down at the crumpled piece of paper she clutched with her fist. Smoothing it out, she saw her name written nice and large along with some other words she could not make out. She handed it to Margaret.

"It says, 'The bearer of this, Winona, is a civilized Sioux Indian who deserves the gratitude of the Minnesotan people.' "You civilized!" Margaret interrupted herself. "I think not!"

"Oh, keep reading," Winona said testily.

"All right, all right," Margaret answered, "'. . . who deserves the gratitude of the Minnesotan people for being instrumental in saving the lives of white women and children, during the Indian War. I recommend her to the kind consideration and attentions of all citizens of the United States.'" Then Margaret sighed. "It's signed by Colonel Flandreau."

"What does it mean? Consideration? Kindness? Civilized? Instrumental? I don't understand." Winona folded the paper as she questioned Margaret.

"I don't understand it either, but it might save your life. Best keep it in your leather bag. Maybe you should move your bag to your neck, so you can access it easier." Margaret wondered aloud. "Should we show this to Mother? To the Widow Shaw?"

"No. If you don't mind, let's just keep this between us and the good Colonel Flandreau." Winona answered. Puzzling over the strangeness of the document and what it meant, they walked to the widow's house on Walnut Street in quiet.

Chapter 23

Newspapers

AFTER SUPPER, WINONA TRIED AGAIN to figure out what to do. Town made her claustrophobic. She wished to be out on the prairie where she could breathe. Margaret, on the other hand, felt safe in Mankato. There were no signs of battle, no burned crops anywhere. Winona agreed that the lack of destruction was much better. She swore the buildings made the wind stop before it got into town. The air tasted stale. Out on the prairie breezes were fresh and new, not having been breathed in and out by hundreds of townsfolk. Margaret laughed at Winona's thoughts, and both girls fell silent, sitting on the porch watching the sunset.

If Winona was honest with herself, she had no wish to go back out to the prairie right now. Settlers and soldiers were still dying, and the destruction they had barely escaped was still happening. It was just so darn hard to breathe, and not to run, for days at a time. It was driving her mad with pent up energy.

Margaret distracted her by reading the newspaper. One reporter in particular was very angry about how long Sibley had taken to get west and engage the Dakota warriors in battle. Sibley was occupying Fort Ridgley, "That's where Joseph is" interrupted Winona.

When Sibley did mount an attack, his men followed the Dakota but never got close enough to engage in battle. "He's scared of a fair fight!" Winona said as Margaret read aloud. The worst was what had happened at Birch Coulee. Sibley had sent out soldiers. They were attacked, but Sibley did not come to their aid when the fort heard the sounds of guns firing. "Why would he not send the rest of his men to protect and back up the others?" Margaret questioned.

"He couldn't!" Winona answered, "That is exactly what the Dakota wanted him to do. They had the fort surrounded, I'm sure of it. They hoped Sibley would send all of his men out on the prairie. The Dakota would have cut them off from the big guns and wiped all of them out."

"Oh," Margaret remembered. "Still it seems hurtful to abandon your men like that."

"He should never have sent them. He knows how the Dakota fight. He should have waited. Sibley's traded with us for a very long time. "

One reporter, Jane Grey Swisshelm, accused Sibley of being a corpse himself as he moved so slowly. Winona chuckled at that line. "I'd like to meet her!"

Margaret was relieved that Winona continued to pretend she was mixed-blood, and with her dresses, bonnet, and pinned hair underneath, she fooled most. They walked around town together every day. Mankato got used to seeing them. They visited the fortifications daily to see if any of the mixed-blood men had come back with news.

Colonel Flandreau was adamant, as was her mother and the Widow Shaw, that they needed to wait for a while until things calmed down more. That was all well and good, but Winona was looking more and more ill as the reports came in of Dakota raiding more innocent civilians and killing women and children. The newspapers carried numbers of bodies that Sibley and his men were burying. They had reached over 190, with no signs of stopping.

The townspeople in Mankato, many of whom had never witnessed any fighting, were now demanding Dakota blood and revenge. The Dakota had lost, they were saying, and all Sibley was doing was burying the dead. The Dakota continued to pull back and away from his army. They would not challenge a real set of fighters. Instead, they preyed on the weak and defenseless.

This kind of conversation was fueled by the rumors that came in daily with travelers. Many of these travelers had come from the east and were only saying things printed in the St. Paul papers. Margaret pointed out that very little of it could be true, as the fighting was in the west. But besides her small household, no one else was listening to Margaret or Winona.

The *Mankato Weekly Record* published stories about the Dakota. Most of the stories were rumor and hearsay but one issue in particular was terribly upsetting. It called for the extermination of all Dakota in Minnesota. Governor Ramsey himself wrote that:

"The Sioux Indians of Minnesota must be exterminated or driven forever beyond the borders of our state. The public safety of our state requires it, justice calls for it, the blood of the murdered cries to heaven for vengeance on those assassins of women and children. They have proven to follow no laws, bound by no moral or social restraints. They have destroyed the very pledge on which it was possible to found hope of ultimate reconciliation. They must be regarded and treated at outlaws."

Margaret was glad that Winona preferred to listen to her read the paper rather than try to read it herself. She was very demanding in that Margaret had to read it to her and help her understand what every article was saying. Margaret tried not to use all the awful words Governor Ramsey said, but the intent of his message was understood perfectly by Winona.

After hearing the governor's words, she went into a very sad state. Winona voiced her concerns that no one would ever learn how the Dakota had been driven to this by the greed of the traders, the government and the very settlers who stole Dakota land. No one would ever learn the truth. They would only retaliate on all Dakota for what the warriors had done.

Margaret wondered if Sibley would follow the order. "Does he have to? Sibley has relatives who are half Dakota. Does Governor Ramsey have the power to order Sibley to exterminate all Dakota?"

"Maybe that's why he's moving so slow. He didn't follow his earlier order to move as quickly as possible. Perhaps he's moving slowly to give the Dakota time to escape further west? Perhaps there's hope for the Dakota who haven't fought?"

Winona interrupted, "He is not a true friend of the Dakota. We call him General Long Knives. I don't think he's trying to be nice. I think he is scared! He should be, Dakota warriors are smarter than him."

Winona heard from the men at the town's fortifications that Little Crow and Sibley were exchanging peace notes. They were discussing peace and hostages. Again Winona wondered if Toayate-duta had the full support of his braves and all of the tribes. If the fighting was continuing and if they had victories like Birch Coulee and Fort Abercrombie was still surrounded why would the braves wish to discuss peace with Long Knives himself?

Margaret read in the paper that Sibley was leaving Fort Ridgley. Almost a month after the attacks started. Winona learned that Sibley had issued a statement, allowing any friendly Dakota to come to him with as many prisoners as they could bring. He promised no harm would come to the friendly Dakota who helped end this violence.

Winona and Margaret discussed how shrewd Sibley was in doing this. He would cause the old chiefs not inclined to battle to start trying to regain power over Toayateduta. If many of his braves were no longer listening, then Taoyateduta was in grave trouble indeed. One can have too many enemies, she told Margaret.

"It has never sounded as if Little Crow had that many on his side during this whole war! Listen to this next part," Margaret read aloud.

"'The Third Minnesota, lacking the discipline many would want in a military detachment, has still somehow managed to thwart another attack on Sibley's Grand army. The men, acting without orders, snuck out before daybreak to a potato field rumored to be near where they were encamped for the night. As their wagons rolled across the prairie, several Dakota Braves rose up from the tall grasses and opened fire.

"'The Third had several wounded men, but quickly returned fire. Others in camp rushed to their aid. Again, acting without orders from their commander Sibley, they pursued the Dakota Indians as they ran from the advancing battalion. Sibley ordered the third back into position knowing the Dakota were drawing them out to attack their flank, but the third paid this order no heed. Sibley ordered again, and was reluctantly obeyed.

"'A battle commenced that lasted at least two hours. Sibley's forces withstood the attack well, but as usual, Sibley did not follow the retreating Dakota after the battle. This reporter says perhaps the Third should be running the campaign and Sibley can pick the potatoes. Sibley has stated, "that the Dakota are finished, that this was a severe blow from which they will not dare make another stand." This reporter wonders if that is the case at all.'"

"How about them apples!" Margaret had to laugh after reading. "Sibley is certainly moving slower than I'd ever thought possible. Here it is late September, and where is he? At Wood Lake? Honestly, could he move any slower?"

"Sure," Winona replied, "He could be walking backwards."

They shared a bitter laugh at this and then pondered their own thoughts for a while. Margaret was struck by food. Eggs and potatoes? This was a war of hunger. The Dakota were hungry and took eggs. This started a war they felt they would not win, but one they needed to fight for self-respect. The war could end now with Minnesota soldiers trying to get potatoes to eat. Was no one well fed in this state of plenty? The land of milk and honey her minister had always described it. She doubted him now.

Winona interrupted her thoughts of food. "I think the Dakota are splitting up. Some will start to try to give their hostages to Sibley in return for promises of food and no punishment. Wood Lake is very close to the Upper Agency. Can Taoyateduta mount another attack? His men have to be getting hungry. Can he keep urging them to fight the forts and the soldiers, when they are not winning?"

Chapter 24

Life Goes on as Usual

COULD THE DAKOTA MOUNT ANOTHER ATTACK? Margaret and Winona wondered this as their lives went into a pattern. Winona had given up on the idea to run through the prairie to find home. There were too many soldiers in her way. But she still forced Margaret to go to the barricades each day to learn the news. School had started in Mankato. Everyone here thought things should return to normal. Margaret and Winona were forced to attend class. Not that either was happy about it. After school, they visited the men in the barricades, then returned to read the paper together on the porch.

Margaret's mother and Isaac were doing really well. Mother was busy all day sewing clothes for other survivors and building up quite the reputation as a seamstress in town. The Widow Shaw told everyone of her sewing, and people seemed to do what the widow suggested. They came to the house on Walnut Street to have their clothes taken in or let out depending on their situation.

Margaret's mother, as well as many others, was becoming convinced it would take years for the war to be over. She knew her husband and son were dead. Mother did not need to wait until the hostages were released for this knowledge. She had no desire to return to the prairie or their farm. "I doubt I can give the farm away to anyone. No one in their right mind is going back out there!" Ma said one night as she and the widow discussed the future.

"I think we need to head east, to a big city—Saint Paul, Milwaukee, maybe Chicago. I have relatives in Milwaukee. They might take us in while I get my feet under me. We have lived off your generosity long enough Mrs. Shaw. I cannot ever repay you, but nor do I wish to continue being a burden."

"My, dear," the widow exclaimed. "You are not a burden. You have given me a new life. I was rambling in this house, all at loose ends. Now I finally feel as if I have a purpose, a meaning to my life. I need you to stay. It's *you* who are helping me!"

Margaret and Winona held their breath. Winona could not go east. Mankato was as crowded as she could stand. Margaret knew this would completely mean the end of their existence together.

"No, we have been a drain on your household long enough, in the morning I shall inquire at the telegraph office. My cousins in Milwaukee wrote back to me and have offered to wire us enough money to purchase train tickets. We need to get back to our lives and stop living off your kindness. Although I'm so grateful for all you have done. I can't continue to put you out like we have."

The widow sputtered and continued, but to no avail. Margaret's mother was adamant in her plan.

Winona stepped on to the front porch with Margaret. "What are we going to do?" she hissed at Margaret. "I cannot go east. Is it time for us to part ways? First thing tomorrow, I'll head off into the prairie. You'll be stuck in Milwaukee. I'm sorry, but I just cannot go any further east. I cannot live like this any longer." She held her skirts to the side and attempted to curtsy.

Margaret attempted a chuckle at the ridiculousness of Winona curtsying. But the smile wouldn't reach her eyes. "We have to do something. And we have to do it quick."

"What?"

"I don't know, but come on. Times a'wasting." With that Margaret turned on her heels and marched off the porch steps. Winona followed, not sure what Margaret could be up to. Apparently nothing, as it turned out. They walked until sunset and then returned home. Having thought of no plan, no ideas, and no way to not be separated in the morning.

The Widow Shaw awoke Winona and Margaret early the next morning, before the sun had even risen. "Listen" she whispered, "I've had an idea. You girls need to get down to the newspaper office. There's a lady journalist there who plans to go west to Camp Release. My neighbor Minnie just heard about it. You need to find out if she needs an interpreter. Then you two can go with her, and your mother can stay here. I've an idea that she might take a liking to you, but I need some time to put it all together. You just can't head to Milwaukee. I won't let you."

Not having any idea what Camp Release meant, the girls hastened to obey the Widow Shaw. She seemed to be their ally to staying here, and that was worth something.

The *Mankato Weekly Record* office was not open so early. But the girls decided to sit on the bench out front and wait a bit. Winona was regretting not getting breakfast. She could hear Margaret's stomach complain as well. Just as they were about to go back and get something to eat, the paper's owner came up to unlock the door.

"What are you doing here so early?" he asked

"We heard of a lady journalist heading west to Camp Release. We wondered if we could speak with her?" Margaret asked, acting as if she knew all about this Camp Release. Winona was impressed with Margaret's poise.

"Sure, come on in. Miss Winston is staying in the back room. Should be up by now, I reckon."

"Miss Winston, you have a couple of visitors," he called out into the empty office. Most of the office was taken up with an enormous printing machine. Rows of cabinets stretched along the wall. A curtain was pulled back separating a small room with a cot and table from the front office.

"Hello, how can I help you?" a young lady said as she emerged from the back room. She stretched out her hand, and the girls took turns shaking it.

"We were wondering if you were the reporter headed to Camp Release?" Margaret asked.

"Yes, I am. I plan on leaving tomorrow morning. There are a lot of folks heading to New Ulm tomorrow. I plan on leaving with them. Safety in numbers, I guess. Why?" Miss Winston replied.

"Well, we were wondering if you might need an interpreter. Winona here is Dakota. She could help you in capturing the stories you want to write down." Winona gaped at Margaret. She still wasn't sure what was going on. Was Camp Release filled with Dakota? Where was this going?

Miss Winston looked Winona up and down and then looked Margaret over as well. "How much do you two know of Camp Release?" she questioned.

"Not much, truthfully." Margaret answered. "We just thought you could use our help."

"I can indeed. The Dakota have held white prisoners for the last six weeks. Now they're free but don't know what to do yet. There's Dakota there as well who turned themselves in with the prisoners. I had planned on writing their stories down, but I didn't know my plan had been told about town."

"We live with the Widow Shaw. She knows everything," Winona said.

"I reckon she must," Miss Winston replied. "I'm Eliza, by the way, and I could indeed use an interpreter. Are you both aiming to come with me? I could use help if you're willing to carry my equipment. I'm also a photographer." She paused and looked at Winona and Margaret.

Margaret and Winona exchanged looks, "We'd both like to come, yes." Margaret answered.

"Good, be here at daybreak or you'll miss your wagon. Bring your mother or the Widow Shaw with you. I'll need to make sure this is all right with your family."

The girls ran out of the office. Winona ran as fast as she could in the long skirts she was forced to wear. They burst into the kitchen and shouted their good news for both Margaret's mother and the Widow Shaw to hear.

Of course, Margaret's mother was not about to let them leave. "Who knows what could happen? I can't bear to lose the two of you after having lost so much!" she cried.

Again, the Widow Shaw came to the aid of the girls in her answer. "You have to let them go. Winona has been like a caged animal since she got here. She has to find out what has happened to her family. She can't rest or settle into her schooling or learn a trade until she does. You know that. You have to let them go. It's a large, armed group. Most of the Dakota have given up. Little Crow will surrender soon as well. Think of all Winona has given up? All that she did for you? Why, you might not be here if it weren't for her. She needs Margaret in this as well. They're thick as thieves and will keep each other safe. You must let them go, with your blessings."

Winona glanced at Margaret, who rolled her eyes a bit with the faintest hint of a grin. She whispered in Margaret's ear, "She's working your mother over good!"

Margaret's mother finally agreed and helped them pack a trunk. "Plenty of bonnets in there," she said and winked at Winona.

Then she gave Margaret a knife. "Have Winona show you how to fasten it to your leg. You may need it."

Mother and the Widow Shaw walked them to the office. She hugged Margaret first and told her not to let Winona out of her sight for a minute. Then she hugged Winona and told her, "Stay with Margaret and Miss Winston. I doubt it's safe for someone who looks Dakota. So no matter how ridiculous you may feel in a bonnet, wear it. It just might save your life." A bit louder she said, "It would be best, though, if you wore it and not just let it dangle off your shoulders."

Winona gaped at her before she was pulled into another massive hug. "Be safe and thank you for all you did for us." She turned then and walked away, but Margaret saw the tears in her eyes. Margaret and Winona shook their heads at each other. Mother sure didn't miss much.

The Widow Shaw talked up a blue streak until it was time for the wagons to leave. Margaret and Winona hugged her and kissed baby Isaac goodbye.

Chapter 25

Camp Release

THEY SET OFF WITH THE CARAVAN moving west. Their trunk was loaded into a covered wagon owned by the newspaper. A lot of equipment was in the wagon as well as Eliza Winston's trunk. There was a tremendous amount of food. Some in the caravan were also headed to Camp Release. Others had their wagons loaded with lumber, planning to rebuild their homes and towns they had abandoned.

It took longer to ride than to walk, since the road was flooded with people. They met some people leaving Minnesota never to come back, but just as many were headed back to start over.

Eliza told of how the annuity money that was supposed to have gone to the Dakota in August would now go to the survivors of the attacks. "Dakota survivors?" Winona asked.

"No, the settlers" Eliza said sympathetically. "The Dakota did what was probably the worst thing possible for their survival in Minnesota. The Dakota killed women and children, 'innocents' who had not harmed them. Unfortunately, the story of why they attacked will be drowned out in the state's screams for revenge. I'm thinking the Dakota might all be forced to leave the Minnesota. Some are screaming that they should be exterminated. Of course that's Jane Gray Swisshelm for you, and you know how she is."

Winona and Margaret both nodded, they had read a lot of articles from Miss Swisshelm. She was arguing for the removal of all Dakota. In some articles she even said they should receive a permanent home, a grave.

"They'll be forced out of Minnesota, to where is the question. I've heard Sibley is going to put the warriors on trial. I've even heard some have been sentenced to hang simply for taking part in the war."

"All of them?" Margaret asked, "Even those who only fought soldiers?"

"All of them," said Eliza. "The list of those sentenced is several hundred names long and they still have many to put on trial. I don't know what's true and what's just rumor and gossip. That's why we have to get there and figure out what's going on."

It took days to arrive at Camp Release. It was further west than both Indian agencies. When they got there, they found two very distinct camps. One was filled with thousands of Dakota women and children, loosely guarded. Another filled with the white prisoners who had lived through the ordeal of the last six weeks. But they could find no Dakota men, warriors, or chiefs, and when they asked, they were informed that the Dakota warriors were awaiting trial. They were separated from their families. They had been tricked Winona learned.

The Dakota women told Winona that the men had had been told to lay down their weapons and to go inside the warehouse to sign their annuity papers and get their money as promised. Since they had turned in their prisoners and had agreed not to fight, they believed Sibley when he said this.

Instead they were caged into the large windowless warehouse and could not see their families. All were waiting for a trial to see if they had killed anyone, who they had killed, how many and whether women had died at their hands. If they were found innocent, they would be released. But that was not what they had agreed to when they had surrendered.

Sketch artists and journalists were allowed inside. Eliza went in to talk with some of the men. Winona and Margaret were stopped and told they were not allowed, but Eliza interceded on Winona's behalf. "She's my translator." They were allowed in.

The Dakota men were bitterly disappointed with the white man's government, with Sibley. Again they had been tricked. It was unfair and unjust. Most of the men who had started the war were not imprisoned. They had not surrendered but had fled west. The men who had surrendered were called friendlies. They had helped keep the white prisoners alive when others wished to kill them. Some of the men had already been sentenced to die, many who had fought against soldiers, but not harmed women and children.

They told Eliza, through Winona, that the ones who had done the attacks on women and children were Red Middle Voice's band and others. They had left. They were with Taoyateduta and the other chiefs who refused to surrender. They had traveled west to gather more tribes of Dakota to help in their fight.

The men tried to tell this to Sibley, but it seemed that few were listening to their story. While they walked and spoke with the men, Winona constantly searched for members of her band. It seemed to be true what the men said. They were not there.

Suddenly, Winona found herself face to face with Watcher, the Dakota brave from Margaret's farm, the one she had tricked at their hiding spot. His eyes held no fire, just quiet disappointment. His name was Rdainyanka, and he was Chief Wabasha's son-in-law. He told Winona, and she told Eliza about the final days in the Dakota camps.

"We had many councils, many arguments about whether we should give up to the whites. My father, Wabasha, said we must. He said we must surrender our hostages and allow the white prisoners to return to their families. I disagreed but went along with him. I said at the Council Fire that I was for continuing this war. I did not think that the whites would stand by their agreements as they have not stood by any they made. Ever since we first treated with them, ever since the very beginning, their agents have robbed and cheated us.

"I said, 'It was not the intention of the Dakota nation to kill any of the whites until the four men returned from Acton and told what they had done. When they did this, I told Council, 'All the young men became excited and commenced the massacre. The older ones would have prevented it if they could, but since the treaties, they have lost all their influence. The young men will not listen to them. They have no power.

"I regret what has happened, but it went too far to be easily remedied. We should have died, and although I am not proud of it now, I said, 'We should have killed all the prisoners with us as the whites will not honor their agreements.'

"Taoyateduta agreed with me. Wabasha did not. Wabasha is my father-in-law. I had to go with him. Now I sit in jail, waiting for my death. Taoyateduta is free on the prairie."

After Rdainyanka finished speaking, Winona knew it was futile to search for her family. But she could not help herself. Eliza and Margaret followed for a while, but then went to interview the newly freed whites and mixed-bloods. Winona's mother was nowhere to be found. Red Middle Voice's camp had been huge but Winona found no one who had heard of or seen any of Red Middle Voice's band. Finally one mixed-blood shared that he had heard the entire band as well as Taoyateduta and hundreds of others had continued to move west and north.

Just as Rdainyanka had said, the best fighters and the ones who had done the greatest atrocities to the white families had fled. The traditional Dakota were not prepared to give up fighting. They had handed over their prisoners to the friendly Dakota who were surrendering and had left before Sibley had arrived.

Now Winona was completely alone. She had no possible way to catch up with her family. They were far out of her reach. She wondered aloud "Do I even want to if catch up with them or am I better staying with Margaret? What am I going to do?"

Chapter 26

Winona's Future Is Settled

ARGARET FOUND WINONA RAGING and cursing at herself. As always her hands were clenched into fists and she was grinding her teeth. Finally it was more than Margaret could stand, and she pulled on Winona's hand. Then she sat her down on a tree trunk. Undoing her hair, she braided it with her fingers, calming Winona as she did. Rebraiding and wrapping her hair back into a bun, she said, "It's time to go talk with Eliza and figure out your future."

Without waiting for an answer, she took Winona's hand and marched her to the tent they had been sharing with the journalist. Interrupting Eliza's work, Margaret asked, "Would you have any idea of work available for my friend Winona after this is over? She likes a challenge and needs to be kept moving."

Eliza smiled and said, "I think I have just the thing. I still need an interpreter. I want to get the stories from as many Dakota men before they are moved away and then from as many Dakota women as possible. I'm good at many things, but speaking Dakota is not one of them. So what do you say, Winona? Would you be willing to stay on and continue working on this project with me? We'll have to send Margaret back. We'll have to travel wherever the army sends the Dakota. It might not be all sheets and clean clothes."

Winona looked from Margaret to Eliza and had the uncanny impression they had planned this. Still it did appeal to her. The story of why the war had happened would never be told if Winona did not help with this project.

"Agreed!" she said. Winona and Margaret had been lucky to have survived. Perhaps they had survived so the story could get written down, recorded for others to know. Certainly very few were interested in the stories of the Dakota side of events right now. Most of the stories in the Mankato paper focused on revenge not on why it had started. But who knew, maybe some day, people would be interested in the truth.

Margaret, Winona, and Eliza continued to move around the camp for the next few days. They spoke with many newly freed prisoners and their Dakota captors. Since they were in two camps, the stories were hard to match up.

The women and children had been absent for most of the fighting but they had been close to the attacks on Fort Ridgley. The Dakota women had followed the braves to a safe distance and set up small cooking fires so the Dakota could eat and continue to fight strongly. The children played with the hostage children, and, although they knew that something was wrong, it had not interfered with their play. They were still playing together, and the guards did not stop them from going between the two camps.

Margaret watched their play, so similar to how Winona and her friendship had started. She did not think many of these friendships would survive the next few weeks. Everyone would be separated soon.

The Dakota wives spoke to Eliza and mentioned repeatedly how they had taken good care of the white women. They dressed them in Dakota clothes so their warriors would not harm them, protecting them from braves who may have wished to harm them in other ways. They didn't make them do any work they said, but treated them as if they were wives of chiefs. Winona translated all of this to Eliza and Margaret but with a wry grin on her face.

Margaret knew that this was not completely true as the women hostages told of having to work all day and had the blistered hands to show for it. They were emaciated and filthy until given the chance to bathe and put on new clothes. Margaret wished she had thought to bring more clothing with her.

The white women spoke of living in constant fear that their protector would tire of them, or think they were not working hard enough and send her away to be killed, or worse kill her children in front of her. Many women had had that happen to them and they were found sitting and staring into space, no longer caring about anything.

One woman both Dakota and whites shunned, a white woman named Sarah. She was the same age as Margaret's mother but her hair had turned completely white during her six-week captivity. This made her face seem much older. The Dakota said she was not keeping her promise to her Dakota protector named Chaska. The white women said she was disgraceful. They said she had fallen in love with him and had forgotten her place.

Sarah herself tried every day to make the soldiers realize that Chaska had never hurt any whites and should not be on trial. Each day that she tried to speak, the whites and Dakota alike further shunned her. *What a terrible thing to do to someone trying to avoid more bloodshed*, thought Margaret.

Eliza listened to her, and wrote much of her story down but said there was too much of it and that Sarah needed to write her own story, that she had to make people know the truth. No one then and there would listen, but later people would need her story. Sarah seemed comforted by this. Margaret realized how powerful the written word could be. Eliza continued to listen and record. It comforted so many to believe their story would be told, that they would not be forgotten.

Winona enjoyed helping Eliza. The journalist was kind and compassionate. She gathered the stories in a notebook and tried to take photographs but seemed to struggle with her equipment. Finally she abandoned taking photos entirely and wrote more. Eliza said she had worked with a missionary before on the Winnebago reservation. She told Winona that people often learned of only one side of an event and it was important for a newspaper to present the facts from both sides.

Eliza told Winona that she should continue to learn how to read and write so she could tell her own story and make sure the truth was told. Many people were going to forget the helpful Dakota in this struggle, Eliza said. They would want to tell it as if all the Dakota were savage and bloodthirsty. Winona would need to tell her side and help Eliza find out more stories like her own.

Margaret and Winona moved with the camps as they relocated to the Lower Agency. It was getting cooler now, and the days were growing shorter. They noticed that very few of the crops that had survived were being harvested. Too many families had lost the sons and brothers to do the work, the widows and children planned to head east like Margaret's mother. Margaret decided to continue with some of the families to New Ulm and from there to Mankato. She needed to help her mother. She hoped that the Widow Shaw had had enough time to put her plan into action.

Winona was going to stay with the Dakota prisoners and continue to work with Eliza. She promised to come visit when she was done with her work. Eliza gave Margaret her card with the newspaper's address in Mankato and said that they would be able to forward letters to her if Margaret wished to write.

When Margaret reached Mankato. She went to the newspaper office first. There were notes and messages tacked to the wall, people leaving messages for loved ones, hoping to find lost relatives. Margaret was overcome with sadness. So many people had died. New Ulm had a similar wall. She guessed every town would have one.

The number of dead would never be known but it was surely as high as 500 if not more. The writings and notes survivors posted were sad, too sad to read. Almost all said they were headed east to St. Paul and to write care of a church. Margaret wondered if the intended recipient would read any of the notes.

She went into the newspaper office and asked for some paper and a pencil. She wrote a note to her father, just in case. She had left one in New Ulm as well. Margaret felt sure he was dead, since he had not turned up with the other prisoners at Camp Release. There were very few men prisoners. Her father had left the farm, armed and with intent on killing Dakota men, and he was known to hate them. They hated him. He was dead, Margaret felt sure, and she needed to accept this fact. Mother had.

Margaret reached the Widow Shaw's home and found her and her mother talking animatedly. Margaret bounded up the stairs. Perhaps the widow's plan had worked. Whatever it was.

Excitedly, Mother told Margaret her plans, "We're going to stay in Mankato. The Widow Shaw has found a small shop down by the newspaper office. Very affordable, good light, the perfect place to sew. I can rent it until I can save enough to purchase it. It will be a small dressmaker shop. We'll of course pay the Widow Shaw back for all her kindness once I am established."

The widow winked at Margaret as Mother continued to tell of her plans. The widow would watch Isaac during the day. Margaret would be able to go to school, a better school than the mission one she had been attending with Winona. Of course Margaret did not mention how often Winona and she had gotten sidetracked on the way to school and never made it inside the building. Margaret liked school but Winona had always found something more interesting to do.

Margaret was relieved about staying in Mankato. It was much better than having to go to a crowded eastern city. "Pa would like this," she told her mother. Margaret wrote two notes to Winona, bringing one to the newspaper office and sending one with a wagon train of supplies bound to the Lower Agency, both care of Eliza.

She wrote that she was hopeful they could all build a new life together and go to school together. There was plenty of room in their home for Winona when she wished to join them.

Weeks later, Winona found her friend at the widow's house. She had a long story to share, and she needed to share it but felt too sad to even speak it. They sat in the parlor with a crackling fire in the hearth as Winona told of her and Eliza's journey here.

She and Eliza had followed the almost 2,000 Dakota on their long trek to Fort Snelling. They were the older men, the women, and the children. The government had decided it would be easier to feed them at Fort Snelling. There was no food, no crops brought in on the reservation.

As they had gone through towns, they noticed flurries of re-building. The smell of sawdust was everywhere and crack of hammers as noisy to Winona's ears as the gunshots of the previous August. However, she much preferred the hammers. Many of the buildings were wood, although Winona saw quite a few stone ones as well. She was happy with the sign of all the rebuilding but she and Eliza had to watch the terrible sadness in the eyes of the Dakota women and children.

When the wagons of Dakota passed through New Ulm all work ceased and the town inhabitants stood on either side of the road, glaring at the Dakota with anger and hatred in their eyes. Winona and Eliza were walking along the back of the wagon train when they heard the yells. The soldiers ran to the center of the town, where the yelling and wailing was loudest. Winona and Eliza tried to follow.

There, in the very center of town. By the buildings that had survived the Dakota attacks months ago, white women were attacking Dakota women and children. They were throwing rocks and hitting with their fists. The soldiers fixed bayonets and were able to restore order and get the wagons going again. But Winona lowered her face behind her big bonnet that Eliza had insisted she wear for their journey.

The townspeople's hatred of the Dakota warriors, Winona could understand. However, as always, hate was taken out on the wrong ones. These were women and children. It was wrong of the Dakota to attack the white women and children, but was it not equally wrong for the whites to attack Dakota women and children? All who had surrendered, all who were in the wagons were the friendly Dakota.

They had surrendered in good faith to Sibley. He had betrayed all of them. The men had been tricked at Camp Release into turning in their weapons to receive their annuity payments. When they did this, they were not paid but put in a warehouse jail.

The men were all tried, and all except one found guilty, even Chaska. They were all awaiting a death sentence to come from President Lincoln himself. Some 300 men's names had been telegraphed to the president for his approval of their hanging. The men who had truly done the most killing had all escaped with Taoyateduta, like her brother and father.

The innocent were left behind and starving again had turned themselves in. They had turned themselves in to a promise of no harm as long as the prisoners had not been harmed. Yet again Sibley had gone back on his word and the government would see his view and not the Dakota's.

After New Ulm, Eliza and Winona had left the long column of women and children and continued to Mankato on their own.

They then went to a newly constructed camp at the river, called Camp Lincoln. This was where the 300 Dakota men were waiting their sentencing. No one knew if they would be hung or pardoned by President Lincoln. Many had lost hope and faith in the whites entirely—too many broken promises, too many failed treaties.

Eliza had been with her when a Dakota man asked to have someone help him write a letter to Wabasha, the chief who had encouraged the braves to surrender to Sibley. It was Rdainyanka, the young man Winona called Watcher.

He had told Eliza and Winona earlier at Camp Release that it had been wrong for the war to start but that it had also been wrong for them to surrender. All would be punished, and he had been proven correct. He asked Eliza to now write his letter and she could publish it in her paper is she saw fit. Eliza had not gotten her boss to let her print it yet, but she would, she said. Winona handed the hand-written paper to Margaret and asked her to read it aloud:

Wabasha,
You have deceived me. You told me that if we followed the advice of General Sibley and give ourselves up to the whites, all would be well, that no innocent man would be injured. I have not killed, wounded, or injured a white man, or any white person. I have not partici-pated in the plunder of their property, and yet today I am set apart for execution, and must die in a few days, while men who are guilty will remain in prison. My wife is your daughter, my children your grandchildren. I leave them all in your care and under your protection. Do not let them suffer, and when my children are grown up, let them know that their father died because he fol-lowed the advice of his chief, and without having the

blood of a white man to answer for to the Great Spirit. My wife and children are dear to me. Let them not grieve for me. Let them remember that the brave should be prepared to meet death; and I will do as becomes a Dakota.

Margaret finished reading, and all were silent until Winona spoke again. "I told Eliza I would come here and let you know what I planned to do. I got all of your letters, and I thank you for the offer to continue living here. I do want to. I want to stay in Mankato and continue school. Eliza has shown me that words are more powerful than bullets. They live longer. I hope you meant your offers earlier and that I can stay."

"Of course, you can stay. Eliza should come here to. That office in the back of the press is too drafty for a Minnesota winter." The Widow Shaw bustled into the kitchen to start on supper and Margaret's mother went with.

"I wanted to tell you that I hope to become a journalist like Eliza." Winona told Margaret.

"It is the perfect position for you." Margaret smiled as she said this.

The girls listened to the fire cackling. Baby Isaac was on the rug in front of the fire, playing with his toes.

"The Widow Shaw needs to be a mother to many, perhaps she had no children of her own, so she could mother us." Winona grinned as she said this. She felt for her knife. It was nice to be with Margaret again. She'd missed Margaret these last weeks. Eliza was a fabulous talker, but Winona needed quiet and time where one did not have to talk but could just sit with a friend.

Margaret watched as Winona continued to check that her knife was still in place. When she did this, Margaret knew the terror and desire to flee were still strong in her friend. Margaret had been wishing to discuss things with her friend and slowly she started asking her what she thought of her idea.

"Winona, I've been thinking a lot, remember how at church we learned of wars that were fought to cleanse a land of the non-believers?" At Winona's nod, Margaret continued. "This war was a lot like that. The Dakota, as we were, have been struggling to survive. Men felt they were no longer men after what the traders and government did to them. This was their struggle to earn back their belief in themselves. You said that Rdainyanka felt that, and when we were at Camp Release, I started to think more about this. I know this was not the ending anyone had hoped for when it started, but it was to show all of Minnesota, the traders, the agents, the missionaries and the newspapers, that the Dakota had reached the point where they no longer felt human, felt Dakota.

"They wished to rid the land of whites, but instead it seems the land will be rid of them. They could not have foreseen this. We could not foresee President Lincoln making a decision of how many to hang. The Dakota could not have known that their women and children would be forced into a prison camp at Fort Snelling.

"I know they wished for a different victory. I know I wished for things to have happened in a better way, but I have been strug-gling so long to understand the why. I think it was like us, running across the prairie. We ran because you told us to, We ran because there was no other choice. We had to run to live, we had to hide to live, and now we live.

"We live because of you. The men followed, attacked, they followed Little Crow's orders because they had to. No one ex-pected the boys to kill a family over an argument about eggs, but that is what happened.

"Just like a prairie fire spreads and burns everything it touches, so did the war, it spread and could not be stopped until it had burned itself out. It has consumed itself, but left terrible scars on those left behind. But in the spring, the earth blooms and the prairie becomes more beautiful than it was before the fire. The flowers and roses burst forth. They grow beautifully from the ashes. So it will be with us."

Margaret stopped speaking for a bit. She let the silence hold the words and toss them around, like the breeze will toss small pieces of dust.

Margaret broke the silence again, reached over and hugged Winona. Then she continued, "One day this story needs to be written down, our struggle to survive. But will anyone believe that it started over eggs and ended with potatoes?"

Winona glanced at Baby Isaac, chortling happily to his toes. She rubbed the handle of her knife. Then she said, "People believe what they wish to, but the stories need to be told."

Author's Note:

This story has been a long time in writing. I have been obsessed with the Dakota War since I was a young girl. My father told me about the conflict, while we visited a fallen down collection of buildings, called Fort Abercrombie. The highway cuts through it now. It looks a little like it might have but the sounds of cars are hard to drown out. While we were there, we read about how children had to go down to the creek to get water for the fort because children were too short to be seen above the brush and would, therefore, not as likely be shot. I was struck by that. How would a mother feel? How would the child feel? That story stayed with me.

The Dakota were similar to many tribes out west. They were forced onto smaller and smaller pieces of land through treaties with the United States Government. Smaller tracts of land meant less to hunt, less land to graze their ponies on. Each time there was a treaty, the Indian agents and fur traders would skim off large amounts of the money to pay off "debts" that the Dakota had run up during the leaner years of the fur trade. The Fur Traders would "give" goods on credit and then, after the winter hunting, the Dakota would pay off their debt with furs. Since the traders kept the records and this entire system was new to the Dakota, much cheating occurred, and large amounts of money were owed to traders from Dakota.

When the Dakota made their last treaties with the United States they were promised yearly payments in gold, goods, schools, and food. They became increasingly dependent on this payment as their hunting land become smaller and smaller. As settlers moved into the land and started farming, they also took game and fish, leaving even less for the Dakota. In 1861 a terrible drought again limited what food could be put aside for the coming winter. The summer of 1862 promised to have a good harvest, but the money from the government was late and the agents refused to open and distribute the food that had come before the gold. Congress, in the midst of the Civil War, argued whether they could send paper money or if the Dakota would only accept gold. Goods and gold had usually been distributed together, but in these desperate days of hunger and national war, the agents allowed some food to be distributed but not enough.

The Dakota felt as if they were being forced to give up their way of life as well as their land. Some chose to do this and became farm Dakota, but when money and goods were late anyway and the agents spoke to them as if they were animals instead of people, it became too much. Chief Taoyateduta, also known as Little Crow, thought they could not possibly win a war if it dragged out. It would need to be quick and targeted at the soldiers. However, many of Dakota's frustration with the whites, the U.S. government, the traders, and their own elders bubbled over, and the young men were hard to lead or control. It was a hot summer. They were hungry and tired of being treated as sub-human.

This war was the first in the wars of the West. It is often forgotten due to the fact that the Civil War was taking up so much of the nation's energies and attention. All of the wars in the West ended in forcing Native Americans onto smaller reservations, in most cases away from their traditional lands. And this after large losses of life due to the fighting and later hunger and disease. They also in most cases lost their traditional way of life.

This war was one of the saddest chapters in Minnesota history.

Questions for Discussion

1)   Many war and conflict stories are told from the view point of the boys and men in the struggle. Yet, women and children are always caught in conflict. This book attempts to tell the story of the war and those struggling to survive. How does it compare to other books about war? What did you like? What would you have added or left out?

2)   The Dakota and the settlers view the land and how to work it differently. This created tremendous conflict and set up terrible outcomes through treaties and the US government's mission to educate and change Native Americans. What conflicting viewpoints about things like this do we still have today?

3)   Winona makes a decision to warn and then get her friends to safety. She did not know it would mean never seeing her family again. Do you think if she had known this, she would have made the same decision? What would you have done?

4)   Have you ever had a friendship like that of Margaret and Winona? Is it possible to keep a friendship when there are so many differences? Will Margaret and Winona be able to stay friends?

5)   If you had to abandon your home as Margaret did, what would you carry with you? Why?

6)   Think about other stories you've read involving a close friendship. What role did the friendship play in that book? How does it compare to the friendship in *War on the Prairie*?

7)   At various points, greed comes into the story. Why did the author have Winona and Margaret think about greed so much?

8)   What do you think will happen to Margaret and Winona as they grow older? Do you think Winona will be able to become a journalist?

9)   So many of the casualties in this war were innocent of the causes. Is this always the case in a fight, do you think?

There is a lot to learn about the Dakota War. The Minnesota Historical Society is a good place to start for stories and facts.

Minnesota Historical
Society Library

Historic Fort Snelling
MHS Website